Surviving the Secret

Surviving the Secret

Pamela Vredevelt &
Kathryn Rodriguez

Foreword by Paul D. Meier

Power Books

Fleming H. Revell Company
Old Tappan, New Jersey

Unless otherwise identified, Scripture quotations are from the HOLY BIBLE: NEW INTERNATIONAL VERSION. Copyright © 1973, 1978 by the International Bible Society. Used by permission of Zondervan Bible Publishers.

Scripture quotations identified NAS are from the New American Standard Bible, © The Lockman Foundation 1960, 1962, 1963, 1968, 1971, 1972, 1973, 1975, 1977.

Verses marked TLB are taken from *The Living Bible,* Copyright 1971 by Tyndale House Publishers, Wheaton, Ill. Used by permission.

Charts from *Betrayal of Innocence,* by David Peters, copyright 1986; used by permission of Word Books, publisher, Waco, Texas.

Library of Congress Cataloging-in-Publication Data
Vredevelt, Pam W., date
  Surviving the secret.

  1. Child molesting—Religious aspects—Christianity.
2. Sexually abused children—Care—United States.
3. Sexually abused children—United States—Psychology.
4. Child molesters—United States—Psychology.
I. Rodriguez, Kathryn. II. Title.
HQ72.U53V74 1987   362.7'044   87-16560
ISBN 0-8007-5333-X

Copyright © 1987 by Pamela Vredevelt and Kathryn Rodriguez
Published by the Fleming H. Revell Company
Old Tappan, New Jersey 07675
Printed in the United States of America

CONTENTS

Foreword   11

PART I: VICTIMIZATION

1 "I Thought I Was the Only One"   15
2 "How Do I Know If I'm a Victim?"   25

PART II: OFFENDING

3 Recognizing Offender Behavior   43
4 Recognizing Offender Thinking   57
5 How Do Offenders Groom Their Victims?   69

PART III: RESCUING

6 "Why Didn't Anyone Try to Save Me?"   79
7 Surviving the Betrayal of Childhood   95

PART IV: MOVING BEYOND VICTIMIZATION

8   Giving Yourself the Right to Grieve   111
9   Airing the Wounds   125
10 Getting the Big Picture   141
11 The Road of Healing   155

PART V: RESPONSIBLE CARING

12 Counsel for Loved Ones   169
13 What About the Christian Offender?   189

Appendix I: Relaxation Exercises   205
Appendix II: Resource List   209
Source Notes   213

To all the victims of sexual abuse who have risked sharing their past. Thank you for teaching me about courage and God's almighty healing power. Also to my daughter, Jessie, who I pray will never be sexually offended.

PAMELA WALKER VREDEVELT

To all the mothers like mine, who believed when their daughters shared their ''secret.''

KATHRYN RODRIGUEZ

Acknowledgments

We would like to say thank you to several people who have helped us complete this book.

Thank you, John and Rocky, for your enthusiastic support and patience. You are wonderful husbands, and we love you.

Thank you, Bill and Fleming H. Revell, for being excited about helping victims of abuse. We're asking God to bless you.

Thank you, Betty, for going beyond the call of duty to help us with the paperwork as the manuscript was written. We appreciate you.

Thank you, Carol Clifton, Randy Alcorn, Rodger Bufford, Nancy Marshall, and Ted Roberts, for your warm encouragement and wise counsel. We thank God for you.

FOREWORD

As improbable as it sounds to some victims of childhood sexual abuse, there is hope for their recovery—for theirs and for that of their abusers. God loves them both. One of them needs to bear the consequences of his sin, and the other often needs to realize that he or she should bear no guilt for the abuse. Beyond that, both need healing for traumatic experiences from the past, for most abusers were also abused themselves as children. They have not committed these acts in a vacuum.

This book addresses the heartrending problems of abused and abuser, showing empathy for both, while standing strong not only for help for the abuser but punishment as well. Pam Vredevelt and Kathy Rodriguez have written a much needed book that covers nearly all aspects of the sexually abused child's nightmare. Without help, that nightmare will haunt the abused for a lifetime. Through this book, however, an abused person can find help that will change those underlying volatile thoughts and feelings to ones of peace.

Over the last ten years, our clinic has treated hundreds of victims, both males and females, of sexual abuse—including incest. Many were from Christian families. They were originally hospitalized because of deep depression. After several months of in-patient hospital treatment and counseling, most are now living normal lives, free from the traumatic memories and resulting inappropriate behaviors and responses those stressful events have caused them through the years.

We have also treated many children who were the victims of

sexual abuse—including suggestive talk or literature, touching, fondling, stimulation, and rape—while being cared for in a day-care center. We advise all parents that, if nonparental child care is truly necessary (which many times it is not), to make sure you know well and have reason to thoroughly trust each and every person who has anything to do with the care of your children.

In today's world, research shows that at least one out of twenty adult females and one out of fifty adult males have been victims of sexual abuse while growing up. Many studies show these percentages to be much higher.

While many things can be done to prevent child abuse, there truly is hope, proven hope, for its victims to go on to "survive the secret" and to lead happy and healthy lives. Victims need proper counseling that involves openly sharing "the awful secret," working through all the hidden emotions and confusion that it has caused, learning to take hold of life as an initiator of good things rather than as a victim of bad ones, and then forgiving the abuser and those who might have been passively involved in allowing the abuse to happen.

Forgiveness needs to be offered, even if that person or persons don't deserve forgiveness. For unforgiveness leads only to bitterness that hurts not the abuser, but the abused. Pam Vrede-velt and Kathy Rodriguez in their practice and we at the Minirth-Meier Clinic have found these steps necessary but effective so that survivors of child abuse can truly say, "Because of the Lord's great love we are not consumed, for his compassions never fail. They are new every morning; great is your faithfulness" (Lamentations 3:22, 23).

PAUL D. MEIER, M.D.

12

part one

VICTIMIZATION

one

"I Thought I Was the Only One"

"I GREW UP BELIEVING THAT I WAS THE ONLY ONE WITH this problem," Norma shared tentatively. "I never told anyone, because I was afraid people wouldn't believe me, much less understand. I remember hearing Dad say, 'No one will believe you, if you say anything. So don't say a word. . . . If you do, I'll have to go to jail, our family will be destroyed, and it will be all *your* fault.'

"I really *did* believe it was all my fault. In the back of my mind I was convinced that somehow I had asked for it. I felt sure this didn't happen to other people. After all, my dad was a fine Christian man. He went to church every Sunday, sang in the choir, and looked like the clean-cut, all-American good old Joe.

"It all started when I was five years old. When Dad tucked me in at night, he whispered, 'This is our "special time" together, and you are my precious little princess.' He usually rubbed my arms and legs to help me get warm when I was between the cold sheets. Then his hands wandered further up my legs, until finally his fingers went inside my panties.

"I remember the first time it happened. It's kind of like a snapshot in my mind. I had almost fallen asleep. But when I felt his hand inside my underwear, I jerked away, saying 'Dad, I don't like that! Don't do it anymore.' He promised me he wouldn't and quietly crept out of the room. He never kept his promise. It happened again . . . and again. . . .

"When I was twelve and started developing physically, Dad became very jealous. He didn't let me have boys as friends. They could not call me more than once, and he made sure they didn't. Whenever I talked to a boy on the telephone, he went to the extension and rudely interrupted our conversation, saying 'I'm expecting an important call. This is not a convenient time for you to talk.' Needless to say, the boys never called back.

"One friend, Kevin, worked up enough courage to come to my house. Dad met him at the door and told him I wasn't home. Later, when we had our 'special' time together, he said, 'Boys are only after one thing. I'm just trying to protect you.' Feeling confused, I remember asking, 'Then, why is it all right for you to do these things to me?' That's when he told me that it is the responsibility of a good father to introduce his daughter to sex. I wanted to believe Dad really loved me and that I was his special princess. Now I realize that I was just an exploited toy to him.

"I often wondered if Mom knew what was happening. It

always seemed as if she was sick. Most of the time she stayed in her darkened bedroom, for days on end, with migraine headaches. When she ventured outside her four walls to spend time with the rest of the family, she was very quiet. Dad ruled the house, and Mom jumped to his commands. As a strict disciplinarian Dad beat my brother whenever he did something wrong. Mom didn't say much about the beatings or about Dad's 'special' times with me. She seemed like a prisoner in her own little world.

"When I was thirteen, Dad had intercourse with me for the first time. We were in the living room, watching television together. Mom was in her bedroom with one of her headaches, and my brother was at a friend's house, due home any minute.

"As my father's hands began to stroke me, I could tell he was getting more excited than usual. He seemed to be breathing harder. Whispering softly in my ear, he said, 'Don't be afraid. I won't hurt you. You'll like this.' Then he made me lie on the carpet, while he pulled down my jeans and underwear. I remember being surprised when he fumbled with his own clothes, too. This was something new. He had never taken off his clothes before, and by this time he was very aroused. I felt scared.

"I panicked, thinking, *What if my brother walks in and catches us?* Dad hurriedly entered me with a forceful thrust. I felt as if he had ripped me apart. It ended quickly, but I bled for several hours, and the pain lasted a long time. Dad quickly fidgeted with his clothes, left the room, and never looked back.

"My brother came home right afterwards and sensed that something was wrong with me, but never said anything. I was afraid to tell. I remember curling up on my bed, in the corner of my room, crying and thinking I must be a terrible daughter for Dad to hurt me this way.

"I wish all this was a bad dream and that these terrible flashbacks would disappear. It has been twenty years, but the shame is just as real as if it happened yesterday. Every day a reminder seems to cross my path.

"My husband thinks there's something wrong with me, because I don't enjoy sex. But the thought of it turns my stomach. I feel so guilty. When my husband holds me, it reminds me of my father touching me. I enjoy being hugged and caressed, but somehow I feel guilty, because my father did those things to me, too. I have so many conflicting feelings.

"My marriage isn't the only relationship this affects. It's really hard for me to make friends and to trust people. I guess I fear that when they get to know me, they won't like me.

"This is so difficult for me to share with you, but I had to tell someone. When my daughter, Carrie, came home yesterday and told me Mr. Sims had tried to pull down her panties in the bathroom, I came unglued. That unleashed a flood of horrendous memories in my mind. I feel as if it's happening all over again, and I don't know what to do.

"I know Carrie was terribly frightened. I feel so helpless and partly responsible for what happened. It's as if Mr. Sims tried to take advantage of two little girls: Carrie and me. There's no doubt in my mind that she's telling the truth. I know!"

Unfortunately, thousands of women have stories similar to Norma's. Conservative estimates of sexual abuse range from 45,000[1] to 500,000[2] incidents per year, for victims under the age of fourteen. A recent random survey of 900 homes in the San Francisco area showed that nearly 40 percent of the women interviewed had been sexually molested before the age of eighteen.[3] Approximately 1 million American women have experienced incestuous relations with their fathers[4] and the statistics go even higher when we include cases involving other family members, such as grandfathers, uncles, stepfathers, siblings, and mothers.[5]

Though no reliable statistics exist, recent self-report research suggests that incestuous victimization other than father-daughter exists. The rate of male victimization approximates the rate for females. In most cases the offender is a family member. Sibling incest appears to be more prevalent than any other type. A rarer form of incest involves the mother-child relationship. Still rarer forms that have been reported include uncle-niece, uncle-nephew, grandfather-granddaughter and grandmother-granddaughter.[6] In addition, research testifies that nearly 50 percent of sex offenders are members of the victim's own family, and the other 50 percent are nonfamily members acquainted with the child.[7]

Because society has fought long and hard to keep sex abuse out of its awareness, victims who speak out have fought an uphill battle. Often children have had to tell their stories numerous times to skeptical adults. Added to that, even the Christian community has made it hard for adult victims to come out of hiding. Whether offered flippantly or from a sincere heart, pat solutions such as "You need to forgive and forget" have hindered the healing process for many hurting people.

But attitudes *have* begun to change, and aided by some unsung heroes (caring pastors, teachers, counselors, social workers, families and friends) courageous adults who were molested as children have spoken out. After enduring years of secret pain, they have talked about their heartache—across kitchen tables, in pastoral offices, counseling rooms, and in psychiatric wards. Fortunately their openness has begun to debunk traditional myths surrounding this hideous crime.

With the double-pronged attack of those helpers who have responded to the desperate cries of the abused and the testimony of the abused themselves, public opinion has started to sway. Because they know so many cases go undetected, researchers believe these statistics are merely the tip of the iceberg. For every reported case, they estimate as many as twenty cases go untold. Doctors in the Houston area expect a 500 percent increase in the number of confirmed cases of incest reported each year.[8]

Facing the Problem

Finally society has begun to face the facts statistics suggest have been around for years. Today's widespread sexual abuse has become more than just a family issue: it has turned into a societal dilemma and an overwhelming moral problem. Despite the differing life-styles, socioeconomic classes, and religious backgrounds of the families in which abuse takes place, too often victim and offender play out the same scenario.

Trapped in a desperate situation, victims of abuse have feared shedding light on what goes on behind closed doors. They have known that in addition to counteracting the control exercised by the offender they will have to battle their society—including the attitudes of other Christians. Although, the number of sex-offender convictions has grown slowly, it is growing. We still need improvement in the legal processing of sex offenders and in treatment programs, but positive strides are being made to guide those who desperately need help.

American society and more specifically the Christian community have finally responded to the sexual misuse of children with a long overdue fervor. Treatment programs for victims are now established throughout the country. In most states, children are now given immediate care and/or removal from the home, once sexual abuse is discovered. Churches also have finally acknowledged that sexual abuse happens within their congregations and have encouraged families to get counseling.

All over the country, support groups where victims, loved ones and offenders can receive help and hope, are now springing up. For your convenience, a detailed resource list of referral sources is available in Appendix II.

If you have been molested, we have good news for you. When sexual abuse is discovered early, a hopeful outcome can be anticipated. Even victims with long unreported testimonies can experience new dimensions of wholeness and healing when they risk pulling their trauma out of the closet.

What's Ahead?

The chapters ahead will give you an opportunity to explore the characteristics of both victim and offender behavior and introduce you to some long-range effects of sexual abuse. True-to-life stories will give you a chance to understand the losses victims suffer. For those who wish to help others, we've explained practical ways to responsibly support victims.

We have not intended that this book will act as a substitute for counseling or professional therapy. Instead, use it as a resource that informs you about some of the issues victims, loved ones, and professionals need to address. Once these issues are raised in your awareness, we encourage you to seek the help of a Christian, knowledgeable in sexual-abuse treatment, who can support you in the healing process.

As therapists, we understand and know the deep pain you feel when memories of your abuse surface; but it is because we firmly believe you can experience a full and complete healing of your past trauma that we have written this book.

How can we make the bold statement that you can be healed? For two reasons. First, in the Bible, God has said He is our healer: "Nevertheless I will bring health and healing . . . ; I will heal my people and will let them enjoy abundant peace and security" (Jeremiah 33:6). He intends for you to experience emotional wholeness, and He has committed Himself to walking with you through the healing process.

As you face your abuse, at times you will feel weak, but God promises to give you strength. When you are fearful, He will bring peace. When you despair, He promises to give you hope. When you feel like giving up, He will sustain you. When you feel all alone, be confident in this: God promises to stick with you through all your ups and downs.

Second, we believe you can experience total healing from your abuse because many individuals are having success dealing with their molestation in therapy. Scores of victims have risked reaching out for help and have annihilated the destructive thoughts and feelings that locked them into the past.

Many victims have a natural tendency to keep their abuse a secret. If you have been a victim, may we gently caution you against hiding from reality? Perhaps as a child you denied your assault by pretending someone else was molested, in order to push the pain out of your awareness.[9] While denial may work for a while, prolonged use of this defense causes problems. Chronic denial can lead to severe personality changes. When your mind keeps painful realities out of your awareness, thinking becomes irrational, and you end up living in a complicated mess of self-deception and reality distortion.[10]

Facing victimization in a safe, loving environment is the first step to healing. As you take God's hand and face the painful realities of undeserved sexual abuse, He will give you the answers you need, broaden your perspectives and reduce the intensity of your pain. He will lift you out of your human despair, onto a plane of grace, so that you can face your future with joy and hope. Join us in the pages ahead as we assist you in your journey towards recovery. To begin, we'd like you to meet Carrie.

two

"How Do I Know if I'm a Victim?"

CARRIE FIDGETED AROUND AND CONCENTRATED ON COUNTing the squares in the carpet rather than looking at me. With fiery eyes and her hands in the air, she cried, "I don't know what you're making such a fuss about. He only wanted to look at me with my pants down. He swore it would never happen again."

"Did it happen again?" I asked.

"Well, yes. A couple of times, I guess. But it's over now. I just want to forget about it and get on with my life. The only time I think about it is when you make me," Carrie replied.

"Carrie, what about the nights you cry yourself to sleep and the times you feel out of control with fits of rage? You told me earlier that you usually have these episodes along with flashbacks of Mr. Sims.''

After a long silence, she reluctantly said, ''I know you're right. I *do* feel confused about what happened to me, and I don't understand why he did those things. But I hate thinking about it.''

My conversation with Carrie illustrates two areas of confusion for the sex-abuse victim. The first concerns the area of definition. Many who have been abused do not know what actually constitutes sexual victimization. Second, victims are usually unfamiliar with the fact that long-range effects may arise from molestation.

Defining Terms

A variety of words are used in research concerning sexual abuse. However, three more popular terms found in the literature are *incest, sexual molestation* and *sexual misuse*. Let's look at each in finer detail.

Incest describes any sexual approach, including exposure, genital fondling, oral-genital contact, and vaginal or anal intercourse between relatives by blood, marriage or adoption.[1]

Sexual molestation refers to the inappropriate sexual stimulation of a child, when no family relationship exists.

The *sexual misuse* of a child refers to situations in which a child is exposed to any type of sexual stimulation considered inappropriate for his or her age, level of development, or role in the family.[2] Showing a child a pornographic magazine, touching a child's body inappropriately, or allowing a child to view an X-rated movie can be considered sexual misuse. Encouraging a child to be in bed with the opposite-sex parent, when the parent is naked, can also be considered sexual misuse if the child is old enough to understand that this is wrong.

These three definitions may appear to overlap somewhat.

However, we can best distinguish them by the degree of stimulation as well as by the existence of family relationships. While we could accurately say that a child of incest has been sexually molested or sexually misused, when a family relationship exists, the most precise term for sexual molestation in this instance is *incest.*

Sexual misuse also suggests (but does not mandate) a family relationship; however, misuse differs from molestation, depending on the degree of stimulation. Dr. Gary May, a prominent child psychiatrist, gives another set of definitions for *sexual misuse.* He suggests two main categories of offenses: touching offenses and nontouching offenses.

Touching offenses include fondling; vaginal, oral, or anal intercourse or attempted intercourse; touching of the genitals; incest; prostitution; and rape. *Nontouching offenses* refer to verbal sexual stimulation intended to arouse the child's interest, obscene telephone calls, exhibitionism, voyeurism (that is, secretly viewing sexual activity between adults or children and adults when such viewing is unknown to the participants), and the general letting down of privacy so the child can watch or hear an act of sexual intercourse.[3] Chart 1 clarifies and differentiates the five terms we described above.

Earlier we described some of Carrie's story. She experienced a touching offense. When a family member touches inappropri-

Chart 1

TERM	TYPE OF OFFENSE	RELATIONSHIP
Incest	*Touching*	*Family*
	Nontouching	
Sexual Molestation	*Touching*	*Nonfamily*
Sexual Misuse	*Touching*	*Nonfamily*
	Nontouching	*Family*

ately, it is *incest*. When a nonfamily member touches inappropriately, it is termed *sexual molestation*.

We often hear the question, "Isn't it more serious for a victim to experience intercourse than fondling?" Research suggests that the victim's perception of the sexual offense, more than the specific sexual act influences the effects of sexual abuse.[4] For example, some women consider it worse to be molested by their fathers than by their brothers. Women believing this who were molested by their fathers tend to be more seriously affected by incest than women with the same perception, whose brothers molested them.

Long-term Effects of Sexual Abuse

Most of the information psychologists have gathered about the long-term effects of sexual abuse has come from those who have sought to cope directly with the abuse. However, researchers have gleaned further information from victims who had originally sought help for emotional and psychological problems, then proved to have sexual abuse in their background. Although no clear-cut cause-and-effect relationship has been proven to exist between sexual abuse during childhood and later psychological adjustment problems, an overwhelming amount of evidence suggests that such a correlation may indeed exist.

Long-term effects of sexual abuse fall into six basic categories, which we can define by their symptoms.

1. *Self-defeating or acting-out behavior.* Symptoms in this category may take the form of self-mutilation, suicide attempts,[5] illegitimate pregnancy,[6] prostitution,[7] and the abuse of alcohol and/or drugs.[8]

2. *Psychological problems.* This category refers to symptoms such as depression, suicidal thoughts, a mind-set that leads to repeated sexual and physical victimizations,[9]

and multiple personality, where the mind splits into different personages to protect the individual from facing the trauma experienced in sexual abuse.[10]

3. *Medically unsupported physical complaints.* This type of complaint appears to occur quite frequently among women who have a history of incest.[11] Examples include back problems and headaches.

4. *Interpersonal problems.* Difficulties in establishing satisfying relationships with others also occurs frequently among those who have been sexually molested as children.[12] Marital problems are a common manifestation of this symptom.[13]

5. *Sexuality confusion.* Promiscuity, frigidity, lack of sexual enjoyment, and confusion over sexual identity are found far more frequently among adult victims of incest than the general population.[14]

6. *Low self-esteem.* Sexual abuse in childhood has some significant effects on self-esteem. Two counselors in Texas, working with women molested as children, found that 57 percent of the women ages twenty-three to forty described themselves as unassertive, worthless, undeserving, and helpless.[15]

It isn't hard to understand why victims have difficulty feeling worthwhile when we realize that we develop self-esteem in the arena of positive, affirming relationships with loved ones.

William James said that a woman's self is the sum total of all that she can call hers, not only her body and her psychic process, but her clothes, her house, husband, children, ancestors, friends, reputation, works, lands, horses, yacht and bank account. To wound any one of these, her images, is to wound her.[16] G. H. Mead says that in the process of becoming a member of a social group, an individual internalizes the ideas and attitudes expressed by the significant people in her life.[17] In other words, individuals come to see themselves in ways that loved ones see them. The social group acts as a mirror.[18]

When we know that, we can easily understand why victims who have been demeaned anticipate further devaluation. In order to thwart potential hurt from future rejections, they often take an unconsciously offensive stance. They tailor their actions according to the motto *I will reject myself before you have the opportunity to do so.*

If you are down on yourself and struggle with low self-worth, it's tough believing that God loves you. If your past bombarded you with the idea that you were unacceptable, it probably has convinced you.

People commonly think that God relates to man much the way parents relate to children. When children have positive, affirming experiences with Mom and Dad, they find it much easier to believe that God loves them and is happy with them. However, when loved ones tear them down and bruise them, children tend to believe that God doesn't value them and that He sees them as worthless.

Studies have shown that some relationship exists between the way we perceive our parents and the way we perceive God. For example, we know that when we have a marked preference for our opposite-sex parent, we tend to structure our perception of God to fit this parent. Although these perceptions may fade over time, they rarely completely disappear. As a result, we generally tend to perceive God in light of our view of Mom and Dad.[19]

Knowing the root causes of low self-worth can help us understand the complexities of victim behavior. Typically victims feel anxious and afraid of the punishment they feel they deserve. In order to compensate for feelings of worthlessness, they invest their entire existence in pleasing others. For a while this pattern works fine, but eventually it backfires. Victims battle a losing situation, because they can never keep everybody happy all the time: It is humanly impossible. Sooner or later their emotional health crumbles.

Unconsciously, victims rage inside when they feel they must "buy" acceptance. But they continue to strive for at least one satisfying and accepting relationship. While victims work hard to make people love them, their behavior communicates that they don't respect themselves. Consequently, others perceive the abused as being overly compliant and willing to take blame and responsibility for most anything. The sad part of the story is that their family and friends often take advantage of them by not letting them off the hook.

Since victims don't give themselves permission to stop caring for others, burnout becomes inevitable. Is it any wonder that victims often feel depressed and down on life? The very behavior they use to find love actually leaves them feeling less accepted.

Victims also have difficulty forming intimate relationships. As children they learned they could not trust family members who said they loved them. Therefore many victims go out of their way to "take charge" of meeting their own needs. They strive to be perfect care givers in order to put a stamp of value on their lives. The more perfectly they serve others, the more worthy they feel. But the elusive dream of being all things to all people at all times never materializes, and they live in a constant state of frantic activity and worry.

Secular humanists view man, not God, as the center of existence and say that self-esteem is based mainly on the feedback we receive from other people. While there is some truth to this, as Christians, we believe that God's perspective of us is most important. Man's opinions will always waver, but God's love and acceptance never change.

As we turn to the Bible we catch a new glimpse of our Creator's viewpoint of us. We begin to see ourselves as God sees us. Verses like Deuteronomy 7:6 encourage us: "For you are a people holy to the Lord your God. The Lord your God has *chosen* you out of all the peoples on the face of the earth to be his people, his treasured possession" (italics added). You are God's treasure. He has chosen you and highly prizes you as His own child.

Romans 5:8 says, "But God demonstrates his own love for us in this: While we were still sinners, Christ died for us." Even when you were at the lowest point in your life and when you felt the most out of sorts, God loved you and chose to die for you.

Psalms 139:1-4 says, "O Lord, you have searched me and you know me. You know when I sit and when I rise; you perceive my thoughts from afar. You discern my going out and my lying down; you are familiar with all my ways. Before a word is on my tongue you know it completely, O Lord." Not only does God know you through and through (better than you know yourself), He also finds great pleasure in loving you on a moment-by-moment basis. Even when you feel totally unlovable, He loves you. In spite of your weaknesses, failures, and ugly times, He chooses you!

The material you have read to this point is sobering. The impact of these facts may carry a hard blow, but please do not despair. As you take the risk to grow in knowledge and to understand the full picture of this problem, you will find answers and hope. God will walk with you through this process. If you are a victim, be assured and comforted that some other people really know how you feel. If you are supporting a victim, please use the following pages to jump inside the shoes of the victim and view the world as she sees it.

How Does a Victim Behave?

When I first met Ethel, an attractive forty-five-year-old woman, she impressed me with her tremendous energy level. But Ethel wasn't happy. Although she always seemed busy, she felt as if her life missed something.

Ethel was active in church. When people needed help, no matter how menial the task, they counted on her to get it done. She constantly drove her friends to appointments, worked several jobs to cover family expenses, and attended church whenever the doors were open. Her family and friends learned to expect and demand her services.

When I began to meet with Ethel, she was hurried on the outside, but exhausted and like a limp dishrag on the inside. She had fallen into a people-pleasing trap and was destroying her emotional health. To get people to love her, Ethel had donated her services, but that didn't mean that she or anyone else appreciated them. Minimizing her abilities, she constantly compared her "little" talents to everyone else's "big" accomplishments. As she played the comparison game the tapes in Ethel's head constantly ran, *If only I could be like. . . ."*

Too busy trying to please others in order to fulfill her deepest longings for nurturing and love, Ethel didn't take time to consider her feelings. When others weren't pleased with her, she rode an emotional roller coaster. One minute she raged high inside with anger. The next moment she was swallowed by guilt and down on herself for not measuring up to the expectations of others.

Before Ethel began therapy, she never acknowledged these feelings. Her denial abilities were so intact that she remained unaware of her negative emotions and could not see their connection with her circumstances. All she knew was that she felt awful 90 percent of the time. Ethel felt mad because the whole world had taken advantage of her; but instead of risking rejection from her family and friends, she turned her anger inward and constantly drove herself to be better in the eyes of others.

Ethel worried continually. She took responsibility for the actions and responses of others. If she spoke harshly to a friend, she ruminated the rest of the day about how her friend might react the next time she saw her. Although she felt used and verbally abused by her husband, she could not stand up to him. No one knew what really went on behind the walls of her "Christian" home.

Back problems further drained Ethel's energy. Before her uterus was removed, she experienced severe menstrual difficulties that had no apparent medical explanation. Feeling ashamed of her apparent illness, she frequently withdrew and stayed in bed. Although the hysterectomy brought relief, Ethel still experienced incapacitating back pain at least once every two weeks. Convinced that no one understood her problems, she felt doomed to a life of drudgery.

During therapy, Ethel began to strip off the layers of hurt that constricted her. Gradually she recognized and acknowledged her anger towards her husband, children, and others who placed demands upon her. She also learned how she set people up to use and mistreat her.

One afternoon Ethel shared a thirty-year-old hidden secret with me. When she was little, her daddy played with her. But when she was twelve, she realized there was something very bad about his "playful" actions. Ethel feared pushing him away, however, because she felt no one else loved her. Unfortunately, she endured seven years of silent humiliation in a sexually abusive relationship.

Ethel's story illustrates some of the common identity and interpersonal problems victims suffer. Not every victim experiences all of these, but most struggle with several of the items listed below:

1. *Victims minimize their own abilities and maximize others' strengths.* Ethel criticized her own abilities and overestimated the abilities of others; this left her crunched on the bottom of the comparison pile. She consistently sacrificed her personal needs for those of others.

2. *Victims tend to take responsibility for others' behavior.* Ethel, for example, took responsibility not only for what she said to her friend, but also for her friend's reactions.

3. *Victims have difficulty in achieving intimacy with others.* For the victim, self-worth is based on her ability to take care of other people. Ethel felt loved and worthy only when she met the needs of others. However, true intimacy develops through mutual sharing of needs in a relationship. Ethel kept her needs to herself, fervently hoping someone would read her mind and know what she needed.

4. *Victims tend to think that if they please others, they'll be viewed as "perfect."* They entertain the fantasy that when they make people happy, others think they have it all together.

5. *Victims obsessively worry about problems and sabotage their efforts to change.*[20] Ethel spent a lot of energy worrying; like most victims, she often worried over *what ifs* in life. However, the question "what if . . . ?" never really

has an answer. Consequently, Ethel used up energy worrying, instead of entertaining possible solutions. This fretting keeps victims from taking risks to change things and locks them into their fear.

The Victim Personality

Research has uncovered a unique and observable victim personality structure among the sexually abused. Dr. Paul D. Meier, noted Christian psychiatrist, describes the victim personality style as one with histrionic characteristics.[21] From his vast clinical experience at the Minirth and Meier clinic in Richardson, Texas, Dr. Meier says the histrionic personality can be formed in one of two ways: by the rejection of a father and the domination of an overly critical mother or by a seductive father who makes advances and an overly critical, domineering mother.

Approximately two-thirds of all women who have strong histrionic qualities in their personality fit into the first category (they were rejected by dad and dominated by a critical mom). The other one-third can be found in the second category (they were seduced by dad and dominated by a critical mom). Women who have suffered incest fall in the second category. Women molested by someone other than a family member usually fall in the first category.

In his book *Christian Child Rearing and Personality Development*, Dr. Meier describes in further detail how the histrionic personality can be formed. He suggests that an immature husband with unmet sexual needs turns to his daughter for warmth and affection and becomes inappropriately close.[22] Such a daughter may be singled out by both parents for her looks rather than her character and be encouraged to dramatize how she feels rather than to admit her emotions. Instead of directly acknowledging her fears, the daughter learns to act out her anxieties through panic attacks or temper tantrums.

Danielle was insecure with men. She sought counseling because of uncontrollable anger and jealousy. Whenever a new man entered her life, she believed all her problems were over, until a blowup occurred. Danielle was very possessive and dependent. Her incessant demands for time and attention usually drove men away. Rather than taking personal responsibility for failure in her relationships, she saw herself as a victim. On numerous occasions Danielle became so distraught she threatened to take her own life. Since friends always jumped to her rescue, she knew this was one way she could keep people near her and not have to be alone.

Seductive fathers condition their daughters to believe they can only get attention if they behave in a sexual way. These women highly emphasize their physical appearance, since Dad rewarded it, but they also experience conflicting feelings. They hated their fathers' advances, yet sexual attention was better than no attention at all. Consequently, their future relationships often have a strong sexual element before true intimacy develops.

As you can see from these patterns, a victim is conditioned to act out her feelings rather than to acknowledge and deal with them appropriately. Her chief defense is denial. She will do anything rather than face her conflicting sexual feelings.

Women rejected by their fathers act like little girls looking for a daddy to love them. Since, as children, victims have not been nurtured or had healthy experiences of male love, they are vulnerable to any kind of male attention, even the wrong kind. In their quest for nurturance, they often get into relationships that revictimize and abuse them.

Research has shown that a victim's style of expression usually centers on her need for attention and love. In general likeable, outgoing, dramatic, and theatrical, but somewhat naive and emotional, she seems very open on the surface—often sharing too much too soon. While constantly craving love and acceptance, her behavior is often attention seeking. Though she appears self-confident on the outside, inwardly she feels insecure and apprehensive. A rich fantasy life helps her avoid her deeper emotions.

We need to make an important point. The personality characteristics we've mentioned are neither right nor wrong, good nor bad. Years of observing victim behavior has yielded this information. Perhaps you have noticed some of these qualities in yourself. On the other hand, when you read the last few pages, maybe you thought, *That's not me.*

Please be patient and gentle with yourself as you confront the realities of your past. God wants you to know the truth about yourself. One of His greatest desires is for you to understand who you are and why you behave and think as you do. Proverbs 14:15 says that a simple woman believes anything, but a prudent woman gives thought to her steps. God wants us to take time to think about who we are. He wants us to consider and evaluate ourselves. As we do this, He promises to give us courage and understanding.

Proverbs 16:2 says that all a woman's ways seem innocent to her, but motives are weighed by the Lord. Many times our motives appear pure, until we discover that we do certain things simply to protect ourselves from emotional pain. For example, we may rationalize our "overcaring" for others by saying we want to meet their needs. Upon closer examination, we may find that our giving has a hook attached to it. We are really trying to meet our own needs for nurturance and acceptance.

Jeremiah 17:9,10 states, "The heart is deceitful above all things and beyond cure. Who can understand it? 'I the Lord search the heart and examine the mind, to reward [a woman] according to [her] conduct, according to what [her] deeds deserve.' '' May we encourage you to let God search your heart? Ask Him to reveal truth and to help you move away from denial, towards emotional healing. As you risk taking these steps He will actively be at work in you, conforming your personality to the image of His Son.

part two

OFFENDING

three

Recognizing Offender Behavior

L UCAS WAS ANXIOUS AND DESPERATELY WANTED ME TO understand his perspective. He had initiated counseling on his own, hoping to convince his wife, the Children's Services Division counselor, and his pastor that he was partially innocent. Although he had recently been caught molesting his seven-year-old son and twelve-year-old daughter, Lucas didn't want to discuss their abuse. He wanted to persuade me that he had good reasons for his behavior. For an hour he unraveled the story of his past, justifying his offenses because of the humiliation he had suffered as a child. As far as he was concerned, no further explanation was needed.

Originally Lucas came from a family that his father had abandoned when Lucas was two years old. Embittered over the fallout, his mother had often flip-flopped between fits of rage and lavish indulgence of her son. She smacked him around the house during storms of anger, then smothered him with loving kisses after the beatings.

Lucas described his confusion while growing up: "Mama often came home from work and banged things around while talking about the creeps down at the factory. I guess they were awful. She said they never appreciated her, always made lewd remarks about her body, and called her nasty names.

"When I didn't finish my chores, Mom exploded. One particular time she backhanded me so hard my nose gushed blood. She instantly felt sorry and hurried to stop the bleeding. I cried a little bit, but Mama apologized, the way she always did, and rocked and cradled me in her arms. I didn't like being hit, but I loved being cuddled afterwards. It was nice feeling safe and secure on her lap.

"One day Mama's sister came to visit. They had a hen party for days. Aunt Lillian brought a big box of clothes for me, along with a few dresses her daughters had outgrown. She said Mama could give the dresses to a neighbor. After trying on the boy's clothes, I was curious about the dresses and put one on for fun. I guess, with my blond curls, I looked like a little girl, wearing the dress. Mama and Aunt Lillian giggled and fussed over me. Though I loved the attention, I wondered if Mama wished she had a little girl instead of a boy.

"Every now and then Mama asked me to put on the dress again. I loved those times, because she rocked me on her lap and told me all kinds of stories. Her greatest dream was that a rich man would discover us and spoil us for the rest of our lives.

"A year or so later Mama did meet an older, wealthy man. At

first he was nice to me. Mama put her best foot forward and never seemed angry. She treated Jim with respect and even went overboard doing favors for him. Every now and then she let him spend the night at our house. I think she was afraid to love him— for both our sakes.

"After they dated a few months, Jim started coming to the house when Mama was at work. He took me swimming at the city pool and out for ice cream. When we changed in the men's locker room, I noticed that he watched me undress. One day he suggested we put on our suits before leaving the house. I went to change, but before I could get my suit on, Jim slipped into the room without knocking. As usual, he picked me up and cuddled me, only this time he stroked me between my legs. This seemed kind of strange, but it felt good, so I didn't stop him. I trusted Jim and knew he wouldn't do anything to hurt me. I loved feeling close to someone who was like a father to me.

"Mama eventually married Jim when I was six, and we became a family. Jim provided all the things he promised, but his demands for sex with me increased as I got older. I felt confused about the real meaning of love. To me it seemed that Jim had the ability to turn love on and off like a water faucet. But I never felt as if I got enough attention and always craved more. I remember fantasizing for hours about being a wealthy and powerful adult. Then I could command love and attention, instead of having to be grateful for every ounce of affection that came my way. . . ."

Lucas's mother gave birth to a son approximately two years after marrying Jim. When Lucas reached puberty, Jim turned his attention to his younger son, leaving Lucas out in the cold. Silence replaced the warm affection that characterized their early times together. Describing his feelings over his rejection, Lucas said: "I was glad Jim didn't want to have sex with me anymore, but wondered if he still loved me. In my mind, sexual attention equaled love, even if it also meant humiliation.''

Lucas's story typifies the early experiences of a sex abuser. Many suffer sickening disgrace at the hands of their own offenders. In order to cope, they become experts at avoiding truth in order to hide from their shame. But years of distorting reality takes a toll: The offender's life-style becomes ingrained with twisted thinking and inappropriate behavior. He believes and does anything that helps him feel loved and nurtured, even at the expense of others.

Research has discovered several common behavioral characteristics among sex offenders. Let's take a few moments to consider the nature of their actions.

Typical Offender Behaviors

Behavioral characteristics of the typical sex offender fall into eight areas:

1. *He is self-centered.* He views himself as most important and meets his own needs at the expense of others'. Not only does he consider himself number one in the world, he also believes he is the center of everybody else's experience and that others revolve around him.

2. *The offender does not own responsibility for his actions.* He constantly demeans others and does not admit mistakes or weaknesses. He blames others and lies, justifies, denies, or minimizes his own behavior when caught in compromising situations.

3. *He builds shallow and/or transitory relationships.* He is not able to truly experience intimacy and is usually a taker in relationships. He invites others to care for him and generally remains in relationships only as long as his needs are met.

4. *He uses power and control to manipulate others for his benefit.* Offenders are manipulative and live to maneuver situations so they have the upper hand. To insure cooperation, they often speak of their trustworthiness as fathers. By using vague threats of what may happen if their victims bring the truth out in the open and by promising bodily harm or a family split, offenders can pressure victims to play along.

5. *He capitalizes on the emotions of others.* The offender learns to take advantage of the emotional sensitivities of others in order to control their behavior. He may play a victim role by telling his daughter her mother misunderstands him. While saying something like, "Your mother just doesn't understand what I need, the way you do . . . ," the offender sets himself up as a victim in his daughter's eyes and capitalizes on her unmet emotional needs. He effectively secures her sympathy and cooperation. At other times he may pretend to be angry in order to use fear to enlist his daughter's cooperation.

6. *The offender generally avoids constructive problem solving.* Instead, he uses destructive forms of conflict resolution, such as "getting away with," "getting back at others," or "putting it over on others."[1] He rarely takes personal responsibility for anything. To him, institutions and persons are things to outsmart and the offender takes pride in deception and his abilities to outwit others.

7. *Incestuous fathers commonly repeat their own family background by marrying passive, powerless women.*[2] The offender has a low opinion of women, seeing them as weak and easily intimidated by his power. Often he does not know how to receive genuine caring; consequently he may keep his wife at a distance so that she remains powerless to meet his emotional needs.

8. *Offending fathers tend to overinvest in the family by exerting rigid control over family members.*[3] They exploit their authoritative role by holding tight reins on their daughters and accusing them of seductive behavior.[4] While holding up a peaceful facade to the rest of the world, they may become violent behind closed doors with family. In reality they are ineffective parents, self-absorbed and highly dependent upon family members to fulfill their unrealistic expectations.[5]

In an effort to avoid their own battles, offenders inflict pain on others, as we can see from these typical behavior patterns. Such behavior does not happen without reason; it comes as a result of past experience and present choices and reflects specific character traits. Let's take a closer look at some personality characteristics commonly seen in sex offenders.

The Personality Behind the Behavior

Most offenders caught in the web of incest want the world to believe that external circumstances caused their problems. However, before helpers accept this appraisal, they should realize that many successful programs for sex offenders have chosen to focus on the personality structure of the offender, rather than his environment.

Webster's defines *personality* as the totality of an individual's characteristics or an integrated group of emotional trends and behavioral tendencies. As a person develops he or she forms certain traits, coping styles, and ways of interacting. By late adolescence, these emotional characteristics and behavioral tendencies are usually set and represent an individual's unique, identifiable personality.[6] We can understand personality as a fixed set of traits or character qualities that determine an overall style of relating.

The early-life trauma suffered by offenders can lead to serious distortions in personality. In some ways pain and humiliation have warped their perception of reality, carving voids in their emotional security; unfortunately they try to compensate for these past losses in destructive ways, leading to unhealthy personality changes.

Paul Meier, Frank B. Minirth, and Frank Wichern see the offender personality as a combination of behavioral and emotional tendencies from three basic personality structures:[7]

1. The paranoid personality

2. The histrionic personality

3. The sociopathic personality

Let's look at each of these to gain further understanding of an offender's approach to life.

Paranoid Personality

Tom demonstrated characteristics of a paranoid personality. He was highly suspicious of his daughter's relationships with boys. After a high school basketball game, he saw Tarah talking with a boy on the team and jumped to the conclusion that she had been sleeping with him. Another afternoon Tom saw Tarah and her mother talking alone. Later that night he grilled Tarah to find out what she had told her mom about him. When Tarah said they weren't talking about him, he slapped her, saying, "Don't you lie to me! I know you were talking about me. What did you say?"

Suspicion, hypersensitivity, rigidity, envy, and argumentativeness characterize the paranoid personality. An individual with this personality style sees himself as blameless and always finds others at fault.[8] He also abuses power.[9]

Earlier we mentioned that the issue of power is a major source of conflict for sex offenders. Abusers use their authority as head of the home to make family members meet their needs. Anxious, suspicious, and defensive, they respond with hypersensitivity to anyone calling attention to their weaknesses. An excessive sense of self-importance and arrogance leads them to blame and ascribe evil motives to family members and friends.

Offenders have strong cravings for attention. However they usually cannot acknowledge these desires, because such awareness hurts their false pride. Confrontation with others who seek attention arouses the offender's anxiety level. To reduce the agitation, he self-righteously condemns the mote in his brother's eye, instead of dealing with the log in his own.[10] Offenders also commonly act like religious fanatics and abuse alcohol.[11]

Histrionic Personality

An individual with a histrionic personality can be described as dependent, overly reactive, self-centered, naive, and overconcerned with the approval of others. Often he perceives interpersonal relationships as unsatisfactory, and sexual adjustment is usually poor.[12] He frequently craves excitement and expresses very dramatic bids for attention.

Early sexual conflicts contribute to the formation of the histrionic personality. Because of their own early victimization, offenders suffer tremendous sexual conflict. In childhood they may have learned that sex was a substitute for attention and love; at the same time their early encounters made them feel guilty. Most abusers confuse love and sex and have difficulty distinguishing between the two.

Offenders usually go out of their way to be likable and charming. They may hold the office of deacon or elder in the church, and others may view them as pillars of the community; social appearance is a very important aspect of the histrionic personality. Though socially abusers appear to conform to Christian standards, family members at the mercies of their offenses see a completely different side of them.

Sociopathic Personality

Ted began having behavior problems in junior high school. Drugs and alcohol seemed to give him feelings of power and control. Ted was bright, and received average grades, though he seldom attended classes. After graduation he obtained a good job as an assistant manager trainee for a food chain. However, within a few months Ted's boss fired him, because he wanted to work by his own set of rules. Through the years the same pattern continued. He never held a job longer than six months.

Ted's relationships also suffered. Sleeping around became a popular pastime. Eventually his reputation preceded him, and women avoided him. With no consistent income and little financial responsibility, Ted also became known throughout his community as a financial risk. Though he was deeply in debt and had destroyed many meaningful relationships, Ted still believed the world revolved around him. He rationalized his failures to surrounding circumstances or blamed others for his own shortcomings. He took no personal responsibility for his behavior. His main concern was to make life easier for himself by taking advantage of others.

One can recognize sociopathic personalities by their continual, aggressive violation of others' rights. Typically they accomplish this with intelligence and flair, while duping large numbers of people. In fact, they are impostors.[13]

Most offenders are sociopathic in the sense that they are self-indulgent and self-centered; they cannot see situations from another's perspective. Due to their self-centeredness and impulsiveness, offenders have a hard time learning from experience. Little things, such as not getting their own way, set them off, because they have an extremely low frustration tolerance.

Sex offenders also rationalize unacceptable attitudes, beliefs, or behaviors. They justify their actions by misapplying reasons or by inventing false ones.[14] Rationalization is one of the primary ways sex offenders avoid facing themselves. By distorting and reconstructing reality, they make themselves look right and everyone else look wrong.

One therapist found that offenders are sociopathic, with strong sexual drives and poor impulse control.[15] They have no loyalty to social values and have little regard for authority figures. While shirking personal responsibility for their problems, they justify, project, minimize, and rationalize reality in order to pass the blame to others.

We mentioned earlier that the sex offender's personality usually combines paranoid, histrionic, and sociopathic traits. While no two individuals are exactly alike, we can observe these particular characteristics in most offenders. Awareness of these personality styles can help others understand how abusers view the world.

Inner Conflicts That Lead to Abuse

Although the offender may seem to act from a position of power and authority, in actuality he has a weak psychological base. His past has left him with a deep inner confusion and sense of conflict and the warped concepts of power and sexuality that have developed contribute to his thinking patterns.

Before we can understand what goes on in the offender's mind, we need to consider these conflicts from his viewpoint.

Power Abuse

Contrary to what some may think, sex offenders do not abuse power out of an overinflated sense of self-worth. In fact, just the opposite is true. Offenders crave maniacal control of others because in reality they feel desperately inadequate and powerless.[16]

Research reveals them as socially immature, chronically insecure, and socially isolated individuals who deal with their anxiety by acting it out.[17]

In many cases, offenders have learned powerlessness through early sexual victimization. According to research, many adolescent sex offenders have been prematurely introduced to adult sex. This appears to result in an anxious preoccupation with repeating sexual experiences; offenders tend to compulsively initiate sex in an attempt to gain power and to understand their own past trauma.[18]

Another study sheds more light on this picture. Out of 348 rapists and child molesters, one-third were sexually victimized as children.[19] Abusers generally come from "loose cultures" where children freely view sexual activity between family members or parents.[20] One clinician who worked with molesters over a ten-year period found that more than 90 percent of the offenders he treated had experienced sexual abuse as children. The offenses occurred when they were between five and seven years of age and involved incest, gang-initiation-type sex, coitus, and sodomy.[21]

Sexuality Confusion

Early sexual victimization contributes to another area of conflict in the offender. Due to deep anxiety over early sexual experiences, he has trouble relating to adults and prefers intimate involvement with children the same age as he was when victimized.

Lucas's story illustrated typical childhood experiences of a sex offender. His confusion about love and affection contributed to his desires for sex with inappropriate partners, such as his children. The destructive relationships and inner conflicts he suffered are common among abusers trying to make sense out of their own pain and turmoil.

Perhaps you are acquainted with individuals who exhibit some of the characteristics we've described as typical of the offender. Let us caution you: Most of us display some of these behaviors at one time or another. Do *not* inappropriately assume somebody is a sex offender just because he tends to act immature or self-centered. It is also unfair to presume that someone is an abuser because he avoids solving conflicts or has difficulty forming relationships. An offender differs from the average Joe because the characteristics and behaviors we have mentioned are more pronounced in his life. His actions have become habitual and deeply ingrained to the point of shaping his personality.

The incestuous father, the sex offender, and the child molester are all human beings created in the image of God. Unfortunately, many of them did not receive nurturing or love during childhood. In many cases, they were abused.

The offender did not become an abuser overnight. Specific hurts in his past contributed to his twisted thinking and perverted behaviors. If you are a victim, please take that difficult step of realizing that it helps to look beyond your offender's faults, to see his needs. In the end, it can help you recover and leave your past behind.

God understands your confusion and knows the suffering you have endured because of your offender's sin. He also knows your frustration and pain and wants you to come to Him for help. Let us encourage you to take this step now. Tell God how you feel about what you have just learned about offenders. Remember, He is on your side and longs to help you move out of emotional bondage, into freedom.

Part of recovery involves broadening your understanding of offender behavior and thinking patterns. Now that we have discussed typical actions of abusers and the personality traits behind those behaviors, we will take a look at how offenders think and view the world from their shoes.

four

Recognizing Offender Thinking

As THERAPISTS WE FEEL IT IS IMPORTANT TO VIEW OFFENDER thought processes as a form of criminal thinking. Although we could use less offensive concepts, that would not benefit recovering molesters as much. Victims of abuse definitely feel a crime has taken place, even though offenders rarely admit they are criminals. It is most therapeutic to help abusers guard against minimizing or denying the reality of their actions.

What Is Offender Thinking?

Doctors Samuel Yochelson and Stanton Samenow, prominent psychologists who have worked with sex offenders for years, show how varying degrees of offender thinking lead to different types of actions. These actions range from irresponsible but nonarrestable behaviors to professional criminal acts. Chart 2 pictures their ideas.

Criminal thought processes can be observed all along this continuum. At one end of the spectrum is the responsible person, who works hard at his job, keeps obligations, and considers the needs of others. People respect his life-style. While he may have fleeting desires to violate societal standards, he makes conscious, responsible choices. This usually does not require much effort and momentary deviations quickly pass.

The irresponsible, nonarrestable person falls in the next unit on the scale. Though we could not call individuals in this category criminals in a legal sense, yet they tend to think like those who have been arrested. For Kim, a man in this category, lying was a way of life, and misunderstandings often occurred in his relationships with others. Although his associates viewed him as a defaulter, liar, excuse offerer, and poor-performance co-worker, his shortcomings usually didn't warrant arrest.

Individuals who fall in the center range of the scale have a more ingrained, hard-core pattern of criminal thinking. While their deviant patterns are less severe than the extreme criminals, they share the same thinking processes.

Terry, an arrestable offender, pilfered from work sites and was regarded by societal standards as a failure. Unlike the responsible person, who experiences fleeting desires to violate standards,

Chart 2[1]

Responsible individual	Irresponsible, but nonar-restable individual	Irresponsible/ arrestable criminal	Irresponsible/ arrestable extreme criminal

Terry had strong, recurring impulses to deviate but outside restraints frequently deterred him.

The extreme criminal falls at the opposite end of the continuum from the responsible person. Criminal thinking is ingrained from an early age, and almost inevitably shows itself in recurring acts of crime. However, this does not mean violators continually have an obsession with breaking the law all the time. In fact, their thoughts generally range from actively plotting crimes to intense longings for purity.[2]

Sex offenders fall into the irresponsible categories of this scale. When arrested, they seemingly cooperate with those in powerful positions, such as Children's Service workers, counselors, and pastors. In many cases this cooperation continues only until they get their way. Through reorganizing reality, offenders strategically manuever, control, and intimidate others to get what they want. Let's look at some common thinking errors offenders use to accomplish their manipulations.[3]

1. *Excuse making.* When others hold offenders accountable for irresponsible actions, they make excuses to justify their behavior. Jack said he molested his daughter because he was out of work, depressed, and felt worthless. Others say: "I can't help myself." "I'm dumb." "I don't know why I did it." "I was never loved." "My family was poor." "My family was rich." The excuses go on and on.

2. *Blaming.* By using this technique the offender avoids solving problems. Instead of facing up to his actions, he blames and builds cases against others for "causing" whatever happened. For instance John blamed his problems on his daughter, Sally. He said, "She is always scantily dressed. It's *her* fault I lost control."

As he blamed Sally, John's resentment escalated. He felt justified offending while focusing on her wrongs. John tended to blame others, not only in heated fights, but also in everyday conversations. At times he even made crass comments about total strangers. This was exciting to him because he left a scene unscathed, feeling like a superman.

3. *Minimizing.* Offenders tend to minimize irresponsible behavior. When confronted, they make light of their wrongs and emphasize the insignificance of their offenses. Kevin said: "I only molested three children. I could have molested a lot more, but I didn't." This attitude also filtered into his college experiences. When talking about flunking a class, he said, "I didn't hand in the paper when it was due, but I handed in everything else. It's no big deal."

4. *Justifying.* Offenders often excuse their behavior with elaborate justifications. While conversing with them, you might hear: "If he can do it, then it must be okay for me to do it." "I was so lonely, I had to." "He yelled at me, so I hit him." "No one listens to me. That's why I can't do anything."

5. *Redefining.* When an offender redefines a situation, he shifts the focus of conversation to avoid talking about a problem. A conversation with an analyst who wanted to discover the extent of the offense might go like this:
"Where did you touch Rachel?"
"She wasn't hurt."
"Did you force Rachel to have intercourse with you?"
"She was bothering me."

6. *Vagueness.* Offenders communicate unclearly and nonspecifically to avoid being pinned down. They are

noncommittal and use words that sound good to others and protect them from involvement. Phrases like these fill their vocabulary: "I more or less think so," "I guess," "probably," "maybe," "I might," "I'm not sure about this," "It's possible," and so on.

7. *Lying.* This is the most pronounced characteristic of criminal thinking. The offender uses lying in a variety of ways to confuse, distort, and make fools of other people. Three types of lies are told: lies of commission, lies of omission, and lies of assent.

A *lie of commission* involves inventing untrue ideas. Mark lied to his daughter by saying, "All fathers teach their daughters about sex this way."

When an offender tells a *lie of omission,* he communicates partial truth with the intent to deceive. Tom confessed to parts of his offense, but did not tell the entire story in detail. He talked about fondling his daughter, but did not admit to penetrating her.

Offenders also tell *lies of assent,* which take the form of passive agreements between the offender and someone else. When George was discovered molesting his twelve-year-old daughter, Cathy, he skillfully used this tactic with his pastor. After meeting together regularly for several months, Pastor Jim felt George had sincerely repented. On several occasions George agreed with Jim never to touch his daughter again.

Convinced of George's good intentions, Jim counseled his wife, encouraging her to allow George back into the home. Within a month George was caught molesting Cathy again. After months of therapy, George admitted, "Even though I agreed to leave Cathy alone, deep down I knew it would happen again. It was just a matter of time. I only agreed with Jim so that he would believe that I was okay and get off my back.''

Sometimes offenders look as if they are lying when they're not. At other times, they appear to be genuinely honest, while actually deceiving others. The behavior is intentional, and their strategy aims at keeping others around them guessing so that they can remain in control. Skilled lying like this makes it very difficult for helping professionals to work with offenders. Because abusers have played the lying game so long, they have a hard time sifting fact and fiction. Untrained professionals are easily convinced by these impostors.

8. *Making fools of others.* Offenders find great pleasure in setting people up for failure by making promises they never intend to keep. They delight in duping therapists, lawyers, judges, and pastors and brag about their craftiness in persuading professionals to believe them.

9. *Assuming.* Offenders spend a great deal of time assuming what others think. They use assumptions as a springboard for destructive activities. Ted assumed others didn't like him and were plotting against him, which gave him an excuse to blow up, rob, molest, or do anything else he had in mind.

10. *I'm unique.* The offender believes that he is unique and different from everyone else. What applies to others simply does not affect him. He's convinced he knows everything and can handle things alone. We frequently hear offenders say, ''I don't need people! Besides, no one

understands me anyway.'' Even when incarcerated, an offender may believe that everyone in prison except him is a criminal.

11. *Ingratiating.* The criminal often goes out of his way to be kind and to act interested in others. However, his phoniness has a hidden price tag. He is most interested in what he can get from others and how he can manipulate, use, or control situations for his own purposes.

12. *Fragmented thinking.* Dan went to church on Sunday, abused on Monday and Tuesday, and attended church again on Wednesday. Seeing himself as a good person who deserved to do what he wanted, Dan never considered the inconsistency of his actions. His thoughts and behaviors were not tied together by integrity, and he had divided his life into little, unconnected compartments. Although he seemed a pillar of the community by day, he abused by night. As he saw it, one role had little to do with the other.

13. *Closed minded.* Offenders are secretive about their personal lives and do not want evaluation and feedback from others. Their self-righteous narrow-mindedness forces outsiders to keep their distance.

14. *Victim playing.* Offenders tend to act as if they cannot take responsibility for their lives. They whine, shuffle, act helpless, and pretend that they are too stupid to do anything for themselves. When they don't get what they want, they play a victim role and act as if they are good and others are bad. Such manipulative tactics usually invite either criticism or rescue from those around them.

15. *Power plays.* Tim used power plays whenever he didn't get his own way. He walked out of rooms during disagreements and didn't complete jobs he agreed to do. At other times he grounded his daughter when she rebuffed his sexual overtures. Sometimes he pitted his children against his wife. On one occasion he enlisted his daughters' support by promising them an outing. When his wife told him it was inconvenient for her, Tim sulked and encouraged his children's temper tantrums until she finally consented to go.

16. *Anger.* John used anger inappropriately to get his way. His temper tantrums and explosive reactions created emotional scenes and instilled fear in others. While pretending to be outraged, he manipulated and controlled his children and their friends.

17. *Ownership.* During a counseling session, Steve said, "She's my wife, and I can treat her however I want!" He believed that anything he desired was his, simply because he owned it. He treated people as pawns and also used this thinking error to justify theft.

Offenders' Emotions

In addition to these thinking errors, offenders struggle with two consuming emotions that seem to complicate their problems. Overwhelming feelings of fear and anger make rational thinking and change difficult.

Fear: Sex offenders live with intense, pervasive fear.[4] They are paranoid of being apprehended for things they did wrong during childhood and are also phobic about bodily injury and death. In order to ward off these feelings, they tend to maintain an inflated self-image.

Jack illustrated offenders' grandiose thinking when he confidently said, "I'm the best salesman they've got where I work. If they didn't have me, they'd have to shut the doors. I practically keep the place afloat on my orders alone. Any day now I'm expecting a promotion to regional salesman." However, two weeks later Jack's deeper feelings came out. In gloom he said, "I'm no good to anyone—my family, my wife, or my kids. My boss must think I'm not any good, or else he would promote me. I'll never amount to anything."

Jack misconstrued what others said and did and received criticism as a total indictment of his personhood. By involving himself with activities that made him feel important, such as hanging around those in prestigious jobs or fantasizing about a promotion at work, Jack developed an overvalued perception of himself. His extreme thoughts of both inadequacy and grandioseness were distortions of reality without a factual base.

Anger. The abuser also struggles with fiery feelings of anger. Although anger is a universal emotion, rarely does an offender express it appropriately. Instead, it usually boils under the surface for years. When he's threatened, an inner turbulent rage distorts the offender's ability to think rationally, and a door is thrown open to his violating the rules. Bottled anger propels him to abuse.

Hope for Offender and Victim

When offenders justify behavior and focus on their reasons for abuse, they avoid facing their wrongs and their need to repent, locking themselves tighter into bondage. However, if they do acknowledge sin and repent, the door to inner healing can open wide.

Our experience as therapists has shown that victims of abuse do almost anything to avoid thinking about their molesters. Focusing on offender behavior and thought patterns can unleash vivid, painful, and scary memories. However, if they reflect on past experiences with a broadened knowledge about offenders, victims may better understand their vulnerability and powerlessness to prevent their abuse. When they learn to evaluate offenders, an important part of the healing process takes place, and victims may begin to make wise and healthy choices in future relationships.

Connie shares her experience: "Fear of the unknown was hard for me to manage. However, when I began to understand my offender, my fear was reduced to a more realistic and workable state. By coming to 'know' my offender I learned to spot potential revictimizing situations. This boosted my confidence. Now warning bells sound in my mind when I see offender characteristics.

"Last week my boss, Mark, started putting the moves on me. He acted as if I owed him an overnighter and tried to coerce me into going out for a drink. Because he is known for being manipulative, in the past I had suspicions about him. Everyone talks about the way Mark lies to customers and promises things he never delivers.

"I'm so thankful that I've learned more about offenders. Before I entered therapy a year ago, I would have felt obligated to give Mark sexual favors. But now I know I'm not a victim anymore, and he has no right to pull his power plays with me. He's my boss, not my God!

"I remember something Christ said to the crowds when He was on earth: 'You will know the truth, and the truth will set you free' (John 8:32). I have learned to embrace the truth about offenders for my own good. As I've grown in understanding and knowledge God has brought healing and new dimensions of liberty to my life. The discomfort of facing my offender and my past was worth the peace of mind I experience today. God is faithful!''

five

How Do Offenders Groom Their Victims?

M OLESTATION IS NOT MERELY A CHANCE OCCURRENCE that comes into the mind of offenders in a short time. Instead, they carefully and deliberately train their victims for offense. Observation and research have led psychologists to see sexual abuse as a coldly calculated and carefully planned crime of opportunity in which other family members may collude.[1]

Before the crime can take place, the offender has carefully set up a situation in which he can make the crime happen; he has groomed both family and offender to a state where they will not object too strenuously.

Grooming Techniques

Offenders use three basic methods to groom victims:

1. Triangulation
2. Isolation
3. Power and control

Let's take a look at how they use them within the family.

Triangulation

We may most easily understand triangulation as the inappropriate inclusion of a third party in an exclusive two-party relationship (for a picture of triangulation and how it compares to a normal family, *see* Chart 3). Though it may occur in many types of relationships, it forms a particularly important part of the incest family's dynamics. Incestuous fathers triangulate their victims by intentionally reversing the roles of spouse and daughter. They relate to their daughters as wives, leaving their wives to become potential rescuers of their children. Use of this strategy enables offenders to coerce their daughters into meeting their needs.

Chart 3

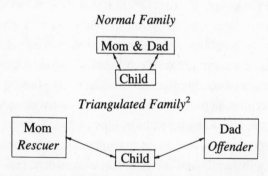

Normal Family

Mom & Dad

Child

Triangulated Family[2]

Mom
Rescuer

Dad
Offender

Child

Joe told me how he prepared his thirteen-year-old stepdaughter for his moves: "I was at a real low point. My wife seemed involved in her own little world and withdrew, sinking deeper into depression. Vicki, my stepdaughter, was forced to look after the kids and to manage more of the household chores. We have always taught our kids to pitch in and help. Vicki was a champ at handling the responsibilities.

"The longer this went on, the more I expected of Vicki, and I maneuvered situations so that she met my needs, too. She trusted me. I assured her that it was perfectly fine for us to be intimate. Even though she didn't seem thoroughly convinced, she cooperated with me."

Offenders use many of the thinking errors covered in chapter 4 to foster triangulation. Joe played a victim role with Vicki and convinced her that her mother wasn't meeting his sexual or emotional needs. In a sense Joe forced his stepdaughter into the position of a wife. At the same time his wife became a possible rescuer.[3] Vicki was caught in a trap between two individuals she deeply loved and trusted. Feeling helpless to change things, she went along with the abuse because neither Mom nor Dad stopped it. She assumed this happened in most families.

Joe was skilled in using this technique. By warning Vicki not to confide in her mom, he set the stage for his wife not to interfere. During the six years this triangulation enslaved Vicki, she desperately wanted to be rescued and assumed her mother knew what was going on but chose not to stop it.

Though some moms are aware their daughters are being misused, they also fear that intervention will break up the family.[4] The secrecy of abuse entraps mothers, daughters, and fathers.[5] If a victim uncovers the truth, she is left with guilt for breaking up the household. If Mom exposes the offense, she stands to lose a husband and the financial support of the entire family. If the offender comes out of the closet, there is a good chance he will lose his loved ones and his personal freedom. As in many cases, Vicki's mom never stepped in to help.

The three roles in triangulation do not necessarily remain fixed over time. Often victims become rescuers in other relationships, to compensate for their own lack of help during childhood.[6] Susie had a habit of trying to save everyone, including her spouse, children, and co-workers. When her husband was hung over and unable to work, she called his boss, making excuses. The kids depended on good old Mom to finish their homework, when it was too hard. When her friends had troubles, she always smoothed things over. One day she even yelled at her boss, after he reprimanded her associate for doing sloppy work. Because Susie hated seeing anyone treated harshly, she reacted to the correction more intensely than her co-worker.

Due to their painful entrapment, victims also often learn to maneuver others to meet their needs. Lucas's story showed how a male victim became an offender. While statistics are lower for female victims becoming abusers, there is some evidence of a growing trend.[7] Offender behavior does not always take a sexual form. Sometimes it is simply the misuse of others to meet one's own personal needs.

Isolation

Isolation is similar to triangulation, but broader in scope. While triangulation forces closeness between father and daughter and separates the child from her mother, isolation breaks the victim's ties with any others who may be able to help.

Bob told his daughters to keep "their little secret" to themselves and rigidly cut them off from the outside world.[8] No one really knew what went on in their home.[9] Because he forbade them to have playmates at the house, and restricted the sports and other afterschool events that they could take part in, the family became a cloistered and frozen entity.

Bob didn't allow his wife to associate with neighbors and friends and fostered fear and mistrust in people he thought might intervene. As long as he prevented interference, he could perpetuate his own distorted thinking and behavior and avoid reality.

Power and Control

In order to feel powerful, Bob deliberately trained his victims to meet his demands. He carried out his tactics slowly, in order to build rapport and trust. As time progressed he took more liberties.

Nancy, one of Bob's victims, tells the story of her past: "At first when Mom went to work at night things were pretty good. I got a kick out of Dad fixing pizza or hotdogs each evening for dinner. But bath time was uncomfortable for me.

"When we were real little, Dad and Mom bathed us, so I was used to Dad playing with us in the tub. But I was ten when Mom went back to work, and they hadn't supervised my baths for a couple of years. Even so, Dad insisted that my little sister and I bathe at the same time, so we could all have fun together.

"The first week he didn't touch us and just laughed at our antics. About a week later, Dad decided I was too old to bathe with my five-year-old sister and told me to get in the tub and wait for him. I felt happy to be grown up enough to take my own private bath.

"A few minutes later Dad came in. At first he just scrubbed my back, but over the weeks he started washing every part of my body. When I got out of the tub, he spent a long time drying me and rubbing between my legs. I asked him if it was all right for him to touch me there. He said, 'All fathers bathe their daughters this way.' I believed him."

In Nancy's case what appeared to be an innocent bath between a father and daughter was really an unhealthy interaction that gradually developed into sexual fondling. It happened slowly. Bob skillfully shrouded his moves in the context of a loving trust relationship so that Nancy wouldn't get wise to his tactics.

Nancy recalls: "I was fourteen when Dad attempted to have intercourse with me. By this time I had learned about sex in health class and knew that what he asked of me was wrong. I refused. Looking back, I realize he had been building up to this for years."

The Offender Cycle of Behavior

Not only do offenders slowly and carefully prepare victims for abuse, grooming them to accept it, internally abusers also experience a compulsive, cyclical pattern that leads to repeat offenses.

After months in therapy, Travis charted his steps of offense during one of our sessions. He told it this way: "I did all right for a while. Things seemed to settle down at work, and my wife, Jane, and I communicated better. But I started drinking again when work got tough and I felt pressured. I stayed up late at night with a six-pack of beer by my side. Naturally Jane wanted nothing to do with me when she smelled booze on my breath. That ticked me off, so I sought revenge. In order to get back at her, I fantasized about her fifteen-year-old daughter, Melodie, who made custody visits every two weeks.

"Melodie was a real knockout! Jane was kind of jealous of her. Every time Melodie made any kind of physical contact with me, I felt as if I were electrically charged. I convinced myself that it was okay to feel this way, because Jane and I weren't doing well in the sex department.

"After Melodie had stayed with us a few days, I looked for times when she was alone in the house. I was kind and worked hard at complimenting and charming her. She was receptive to my games, and before long I convinced her to go to bed with me.

"After we slept together I felt better for a little while, but then an overwhelming sense of guilt and fear plagued me. Questions ricocheted viciously in my mind: *What happens if my wife finds out? What if Melodie gets pregnant?* Each time I promised myself it would never happen again. I just couldn't risk it. But I always ended up thinking, *It doesn't seem to be hurting anybody as long as we keep it a secret.*"

Travis's story illustrates many elements in the offender cycle (*see* Chart 4). Periods of normal behavior usually separate offenses. However, when stress increases in an offender's life, he tries to cope by regressing to fantasy. The more he fantasizes, the more he tends to misread and distort reality. He justifies his thoughts and zeroes in on his victim to prepare her for his advances. When she is vulnerable and powerless, he molests her. After the pleasurable release of sexual tension, he often feels terrible guilt and remorse over his actions. Rather than getting help, however, he explains away his behavior until next time.

Those in helping positions need to understand the compulsive nature of sexual abuse. Molestation can be categorized with alcoholism and drug addiction: As with most compulsive behaviors, the more stress an offender suffers, the more likely he is to abuse.

Molestation has two strong consequences for the offender: pleasure and guilt. Since pleasure is usually more influential in determining human behavior, offenders continue to abuse. Sexual release is extremely reinforcing and drives them to reoffend, even in the face of inevitable punishment. If you really want to help an offender, do not listen to his pleading and excuses. Get him into therapy!

Chart 4
The Offender Cycle[10]

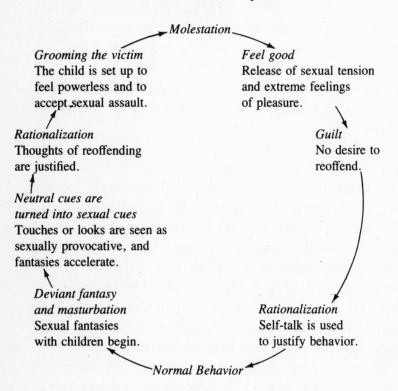

Molestation

Grooming the victim
The child is set up to
feel powerless and to
accept sexual assault.

Feel good
Release of sexual tension
and extreme feelings
of pleasure.

Rationalization
Thoughts of reoffending
are justified.

Guilt
No desire to
reoffend.

*Neutral cues are
turned into sexual cues*
Touches or looks are seen as
sexually provocative, and
fantasies accelerate.

*Deviant fantasy
and masturbation*
Sexual fantasies
with children begin.

Rationalization
Self-talk is used
to justify behavior.

Normal Behavior

part three

RESCUING

six

"Why Didn't Anyone Try to Save Me?"

O NCE UPON A TIME A BEAUTIFUL PRINCESS FELL INTO THE hands of an angry old witch. But according to the legend, everyone lived happily ever after, because the lovely young girl was rescued by a handsome prince. Down through the ages the magical story has been told:

One day a handsome Prince came riding by, far from his own kingdom. He, like many others, was curious about the mysterious castle. He heard many stories, but the words of an old woodcutter excited him the most.

"Some say that inside the castle lies a Princess more beautiful than a summer's day," said the woodcutter.

"If she is so beautiful, I must see her for myself," answered the Prince, and off he rode to the castle.

In no time he found himself standing in the courtyard. The Prince gazed in amazement at the sleeping figures he passed as he went into the castle. There on a bed of silk and satin lay the young Princess fast asleep.

"The woodcutter was right," gasped the Prince. "She is more beautiful than a summer's day. At last I have found the Princess of my dreams!"

He knelt by her bed and kissed her tenderly. To his joy the Princess opened her eyes and smiled up at him sweetly.

"Why have you taken so long to come?" she whispered happily. "I have been dreaming of you for a hundred years!" [1]

Children listen to fairy tales and learn to believe that a knight in shining armor always magically comes to save the day. The sad reality of life is that no one rescues many sex-abuse victims from the hands of their offenders, even when others know about the abuse.

Time and again victims despairingly ask, "Why didn't anyone save me?" How can victims come to grips with this injustice? Who is to blame for their lack of rescue? Brothers and sisters? Mother? Or God? Victims need answers to these questions and doubts.

Mom Should Have Known!

Devastated, Eloise hung her head in shame, admitting her husband's offenses against her daughter: "I didn't want to believe it. For so long I pretended it wasn't true. Mandy tried to tell me a couple of times, but I just waved her away. I didn't want to hear it. Our lives had been terrible before Earl came into my life, and Mandy threatened to destroy it all. At least that's the way I saw it. I guess my own convenience was more important than Mandy's security.

"When I came home early from work one afternoon and found Earl in bed with Mandy, I couldn't deny it any longer. I calmly told him to leave, while I took her out of the room. That's when I exploded. I was outraged! How could she do this to me?

"Everything started coming back. I realized the signs I had tried to ignore during the past year had been warnings. Mandy had begged me not to leave her alone with Earl, but I convinced myself she would grow to love him, if I just gave it enough time.

"For several months Mandy had suffered with constant urinary-tract infections. I took her to the doctor each time, but refused to ask myself why she was sick so often. As I look back, I can't believe my selfishness. I ignored my own child's cries for help. What kind of mother am I?"

What Part Does Mom Play?

Some moms are aware, at least to a degree, that their daughters are being offended. However, to other mothers the facts of abuse come as a complete surprise.

Experts view a mother's role in the incestuous family in several different ways. Some see mothers as a collusive part of the offense, because they believe many mothers know or at least suspect incest is occurring, yet do nothing to intervene.[2] Indirectly they perpetuate the offense. Others, however, recast Mom as another victim of paternal authority.[3]

Clinical research describes mothers of incest victims as emotionally insecure women.[4] They are usually passive and ineffective in handling their husbands' strong-armed authority. In order to cope, they adopt a weak style of interacting with their family.[5]

This characterized Cindy's relationship with her husband, Jack. On many occasions she bit her lip when he railed her two children for insignificant offenses. Later she tiptoed behind his back, trying to soothe them. Cindy rarely stood up to Jack, because she feared he would turn his violent anger on her.

Karen also watched her children suffer from the unpredictable antics of her volatile and rigid husband. He demanded perfect obedience from family members. Afraid of adding fuel to the fire, Karen never spoke up for her children or herself.

The detached style of coping these women used encouraged a role reversal that forced their daughters to assume a "little mother" position within the family.[6] When I met with Lindsey, a thirteen-year-old victim, I saw a typical example of the influence this has on a child. In the middle of our counseling session, she nervously interjected statements like, "Did I remember to leave the door open for Joey [her six-year-old brother]?" "What if I forgot to turn off the washer and dryer before I left?" "I've got to remember to buy milk before I go home today." Lindsey had obviously become the "mom" of the household.

When people outside the home report the incest and the daughters corroborate their suspicions, many mothers don't believe they are telling the truth. In a study of 112 mothers, researchers found that although they denied incest occurring, all the mothers were aware of it and of the collusive role they played.[7]

What factors contribute to a mother's cooperating in the

dynamics of incest? Many of these women were victims themselves during childhood. Parents United, a nationwide incest treatment agency, reports that 80 percent of victims' mothers were also sexually assaulted as children.[8] Other mothers have unresolved dependency needs from childhood, due to parental desertion or institutionalization away from loved ones.[9]

Research also suggests that incest occurs in families where the mother is not viewed as a "restraining agent." In other words, Mom fails to teach her children that sexual abuse is wrong and abnormal. She also doesn't model self-protective behaviors for her children.[10]

Joe and Linda's children grew up in a home in which they never saw Linda defend herself; instead she accepted whatever Joe meted out. At times Joe physically abused Linda when their kids were in the same room. The children grew up feeling powerless against a world in which even their mother wasn't safe.

Many mothers, like Linda, model victim behavior in front of their children. Perhaps sexual abuse is multigenerational partly because of the role modeling victim mothers reflect to their children. A mother's actions speak louder than her words.

Some experts view a mother's unwillingness to stop incest as a predictor of the long-term effects upon the victim.[11] Our experience supports this idea. Many victims suffer more emotional turmoil from their mothers' lack of rescue than from the abuse itself.

However, not all mothers deny the fact that sexual abuse is occurring when they detect warning signs. Some women listen, believe their children's stories, and take action. Others face the horror of discovering the abuse themselves: "It took everything I could muster not to flip out when I called the police. I felt so angry, after I walked in on my husband and daughter in bed, that I thought I would go crazy!'' Tamara cried.

Unfortunately we hear less from the media about mothers who take wise steps of action and more about those who stubbornly refuse to believe their children. We mentioned earlier that a mother's attitude when abuse is unveiled has a big influence on the victim. Mothers who encourage their children to talk about what happened and assure them they were not to blame can be a tremendous aid in the healing process.

Moms Who Care

Linda brought her daughter, Heather, for therapy soon after her husband was removed from their home. She believed Heather's complaints about her daddy's ''games,'' because she had also been molested during childhood. Linda didn't want Heather to experience the years of silent turmoil she had endured and was eager to get involved in Heather's healing process.

In one session, Linda encouraged Heather to express her feelings, saying: ''Heather, honey, you don't have to be afraid. I'm going to stay right here. Please tell me how you were feeling towards me when I didn't know what was going on.''

Heather hung her head and said quietly, ''Oh, Mom, that's all over with now. I don't want to talk about it.''

Linda persisted: ''Heather, it's important that we face these things together. I remember resenting my mother because she didn't listen. I want more for you, and I want us to be friends. Friends share what's really going on inside.''

Heather slowly spoke again. ''Well, are you sure? I don't want to hurt you—but I was kind of mad at you. I thought you *should* have known. You should have stopped it before you did. You and Daddy were always my heroes. You knew everything—or at least it seemed like it, whenever I tried to get away with mischief. But

Daddy made me feel icky and dirty, and everyone acted as if nothing was wrong. I hated you for leaving me alone with him.''

It was hard for Linda to hear this, but she felt the healing that resulted from the open communication was worth her discomfort. Heather's confusion reminded Linda of her own childhood conflicts. To protect herself from dumping buckets of past garbage on Heather, Linda also sought professional help to work through her own experience of abuse.

As a result Linda resolved a deep-seated resentment towards her own mother. After several months of counseling, she asked her mom out for lunch and shared her intimate feelings. She spent weeks preparing for that conversation and carefully expressed her thoughts in love, not in anger. Unfortunately even though fifteen years had passed, her mother still did not believe Linda's father had molested her.

Though Linda felt disappointed by her mother's reaction, she had anticipated her mother's lack of compassion. Linda knew her response wasn't the most important issue. What really mattered was Linda's willingness to openly share her heart and to forgive her mother in spite of her disbelief.

Linda grew in leaps and bounds from that experience. She placed an even higher value on open communication with her own daughter and diligently prayed for compassion and understanding. Through months of mutual sharing, Heather and Linda became best friends and successfully moved beyond the heartaches of the past.

My Brothers and Sisters Should Have Told!

A pervasive fear of men plagued JoAnn. Although highly educated and a successful businesswoman, she felt childish and clumsy around the opposite sex. Afraid her male counterparts could force her to do anything they wanted, she lived with an overwhelming sense of powerlessness.

JoAnn was the "good" daughter in her family, who had made something of herself, and she felt proud that she had risen above her rough beginnings in a low-income clan. Still, the conflicts in her family stand out as vivid memories: "Tim was my big brother. We weren't real close, because he was several years older. I had two sisters. One was a year older and the other a year younger than me.

"One day my older sister asked if my stepdad ever tried to play games with me. I laughed and said, 'What kind of games?' I thought she was teasing me. Then I noticed she wasn't smiling.

"With a stone-cold expression, she said 'You know! Has he ever tried to touch you down there or put his hands up your blouse?'

"I sobered quickly. 'No!' I said. 'Never! Has he done that to you?'

" 'Yes,' she answered. 'For a long time now.'

"I was petrified when I heard this. Several months later I caught my brother, Tim, trying to force himself on my little sister. From that day on I lived in fear. I felt certain it would happen to me, too, and that I wouldn't be able to stop it.

"My older sister wanted to tell Mom about our stepdad, but I talked her out of it.[12] Mom loved him so much, and I didn't want to hurt her. Now I wish I had helped my sisters confess the truth."

Fear isn't the only feeling common among siblings of victims. Some brothers and sisters envy the molested one, seeing the victim as a "chosen one" and resenting the individual attention this child receives from the offender. Often these siblings struggle with psychological difficulties, because of guilt over this "incest envy."[13]

Don't Cover a Festering Wound

For victims, these facts are hard to swallow. If you are one, you may find yourself recoiling in disgust at the thought that someone in your family may have known about your abuse, yet done nothing to stop it. Although you find that truth hard to accept, face the possibility, deal with your feelings, and move beyond bitterness towards forgiveness.

Forgiving your brothers and sisters is necessary. But forgiveness does not mean glibly saying, "I forgive and forget," while stuffing anger, bitterness, and resentment inside. Forgiveness won't happen instantaneously, at the snap of a finger. It is a process.

Most people know that a wise person doesn't put a bandage on an infected gash, because the wound would fester. Although a bandage can protect the surface, it doesn't promote healing. The injury needs to be cleaned and exposed to air for healing to occur.

Likewise, part of the forgiveness process involves victims' dealing with the infection inside their wounds. Cleansing and exposure are necessary. After care has been taken to rid infection, genuine forgiveness and healing become possible. (We will cover helpful ways to wash wounds in a later chapter.)

Forgiveness usually isn't easy. At times we feel the fiery sting of an offense, and find it hard to let the one who wronged us off the hook. In situations like this, it helps to remember:

God loves the person who committed the wrong as much as He loves me. "God is not one to show partiality" (Acts 10:34 NAS).

God forgave me, when I didn't deserve it. "Because of his kindness you have been saved through trusting Christ. And even trusting is not of yourselves; it too is a gift from

God. Salvation is not a reward for the good we have done, so none of us can take any credit for it" (Ephesians 2:8, 9 TLB).

I make mistakes, too. "Yes, all have sinned; all fall short of God's glorious ideal" (Romans 3:23 TLB).

As I forgive others and extend love in a supernatural way (going beyond my own natural tendencies) God promises to return the same back to me. "For if you give, you will get! Your gift will return to you in full and overflowing measure, pressed down, shaken together to make room for more, and running over. Whatever measure you use to give—large or small—will be used to measure what is given back to you" (Luke 6:38 TLB).

We do not have a Savior who is immune or aloof to our pain and suffering. Scripture tells us Jesus was tempted in every way, just as we are—yet was without sin (Hebrews 4:15). He tasted disgusting humiliation. He knows your anger. He feels your shame. He's mindful of your rejections. And He's ready and willing to heal you and help you move towards forgiveness.

Perhaps family members knew about your abuse and didn't stop it. This was an awful injustice against you. However, as you freely extend the grace God extended to you, your burdens will lighten. Once you realize that we are all merely forgiven sinners, it will become easier to look beyond your family's imperfections, bad choices, and unjust actions. Remember, as you forgive, a measure of healing will be yours. God never breaks a promise!

God Shouldn't Have Allowed It!

God is swift and to the point in deploring sexual activity outside the marriage relationship. He says:

Do not degrade your daughter by making her a prostitute. . . .

Leviticus 19:29

A man is not to marry his father's wife; he must not dishonor his father's bed.

Deuteronomy 22:30

Cursed is the man who sleeps with his father's wife, for he dishonors his father's bed.

Deuteronomy 27:20

Cursed is the man who sleeps with his sister, the daughter of his father or the daughter of his mother . . . Cursed is the man who sleeps with his mother-in-law.

Deuteronomy 27:22, 23

In you one man commits a detestable offense with his neighbor's wife, another shamefully defiles his daughter-in-law, and another violates his sister, his own father's daughter.

Ezekiel 22:11

It is actually reported that there is sexual immorality among you, and of a kind that does not occur even among pagans: A man has his father's wife.

1 Corinthians 5:1

You may be asking yourself, *If God adamantly opposes sexual activity between family members, why didn't He stop my offender? Why does He allow sexual abuse to happen?*

Why God allows pain, evil, and suffering is a difficult issue to deal with, especially in the midst of emotional turmoil. In such a situation, our grief-stricken emotions often cloud and distort reality. Because we want to give someone credit for our misery, all our senses look for a scapegoat. Seeing only God's sovereignty, we feel He could have intervened, if He had wanted to. As we grope for pat answers we often jump to erroneous conclusions.

Although most victims don't exactly attribute the cause of their abuse to God, many see Him playing a major position in their injustice. His role resembles a president's when he signs and vetoes bills. Victims see God as one who examines each potential natural occurrence, to see if it has use or purpose. Then He either allows it to happen or vetoes it by divine intervention. Rather than asking, *Why did God make my offender abuse me?* victims usually ask, *Why did God allow my abuse?* Ultimately, it leaves God with a bad rap.

The Bible gives helpful instruction about these issues and how God relates to man. From the Bible we learn that God did not create man as a mechanically operated robot to jump at His commands. Genesis says man is made in God's image. In other words God created us with the power to think, feel, and act. Each of us is a unique individual with freedom of choice.

This freedom carries implications. If a drunk man chooses to drive, he may well kill or injure not only himself, but others. If a mother chooses to leave toxic chemicals unguarded in toddler-level cupboards, her two-year-old may pay the price. Wrong choices affect us individually, collectively, and cumulatively.

When God granted us freedom of choice, it meant He had to permit us to reap the natural consequences of our choices; otherwise choice would not exist. Perhaps it will help to think of it this way:

Suppose that I come to a fork in the road of life. One side is marked Happiness, the other side is marked Misery. Due to some inexplicable perverseness within me, I choose the path of Misery. Now God faces a dilemma. A being whom he greatly loves has made a choice with devastating implications. Yet, if He should quickly refurbish the path of Misery, making it identical to the path of Happiness, He would have shielded me from great pain, but He would also have effectively deprived me of the power of choice. Try as I may, I cannot pursue Misery if God keeps protecting me from the consequences of my choice. I have become a Happiness automaton.[14]

As much as God hates sin (including sexual abuse) and the devastating pain it brings, He must permit humanity to reap what it sows. To be consistent wtih His character, He must allow the principle of cause and effect—a principle He created—to operate. As long as we live in an imperfect, sinful world, suffering will exist. Victims of sexual abuse will bear the brunt of their offenders' sinful choices.

God Is on Your Side!

As they attempt to understand the relationship between the actions of their offenders and God's sovereignty, victims frequently come to one of two conclusions:

God is punishing them for certain sins

God sent the abuse in order to teach them great spiritual lessons and draw them closer to Himself

When they fall into the trap of believing either of these, victims become confused. Why? Because although they may know God loves them, these ideas don't fit that understanding. Indeed these ideas *don't* work spiritually, because neither is true.

Punishment for Sin? Since Jesus Christ came and died on the cross, for the sins of all mankind, God does not inflict us with punishment for our sins. His Son's death canceled our debt, settling our account with God (Colossians 2:14). Once and for all, Christ paid the price for our sins.

Believing that God manipulates circumstances so that sexual abuse occurs to punish victims for their sins belies these truths of Scripture. What kind of loving God would attempt to extract double payment for sin?

Character builder? Neither does God send sexual abuse in order to build character, to make victims stronger Christians. Commonly those trying to comfort the abused offer the platitude, "God has a purpose in all this. . . . You'll be a much stronger Christian because of the suffering." With these comments, such Job's comforters assume God inflicts sexual abuse in order to prepare a person for a greater mission in life. They encourage victims to look at their pain as an opportunity for developing increased spiritual maturity and tell them God must really know they have stamina, since He has put them through this, while promising "He will not let you be tempted beyond what you can bear. . ." (1 Corinthians 10:13).

God's bum rap? Seeing sexual abuse either as punishment for sin or as a character builder inaccurately presents God's Word and His role in the victim's life. If we would believe these concepts, we cannot accept the Bible's view of God as a good, fair, kind, healing, just, and loving father. For how can we accept Scripture's forthright statement ". . . God is love" (1 John 4:8) and the description of love as "patient . . . kind . . . not rude or self-seeking, not easily angered, keeping no record of wrongs . . . not delighting in evil but rejoicing in truth . . . always protecting, always trusting, always hoping, always persevering" (*see* 1 Corinthians 13:4–7), if we would also accept a

God who would use abuse for the purposes claimed above? Such ideas imply that either the Bible has made a mistake in its description of God's character or that He doesn't always act according to that character.

Would a loving and wise *earthly* father purposely inflict suffering on his child, then say, "Come here, let me comfort you and help you in your sorrow?" The thought seems ridiculous! No more does our loving heavenly Father cause sexual abuse, then say to His child, "Now come to Me, I'll heal you, and you'll have great spiritual awakening in your life because of this."

Then who is to blame? We all need to face the fact that we live in a fallen world, one in which the innocent sometimes become the victims of heartache. If you have experienced sexual assault, it isn't a sign of sin in your life or a message from God to "shape up your act." This form of suffering exists as a consequence, a natural outgrowth, of a terrible misuse of God's greatest gift to man—the power of choice.

Because we live in an imperfect world, we would delude ourselves if we expected everything in life to be fair or predictable. Many wrongs never get made right here. But one day, when God makes the final judgment of all sin, He will set everything straight. Until then, we must accept the fact that at times human experience will be painful. We may have questions, but no answers. Sometimes we will have heartaches that are hard to bear. All this comes from living in a fallen world.

At the same time that we would accept this fact, we have hope for bright tomorrows. Without a doubt we know that ". . . all things God works for the good of those who love him. . ." (Romans 8:28).

Some people may read that verse and interpret it this way: *God works pain and joy, good and evil into my life for my good. Thus He allowed me to experience sexual abuse in order to accomplish good*. We prefer to look at it another way: God does not inflict sexual abuse on victims to work a certain "good" or growth in their lives. Instead, abuse has touched them with the pain of human experience, and in the process of groping for answers and understanding, growth is produced. God's involvement with them in that growth process gives them hope, strength, tenacity, and comfort.

As victims come to grips with their anger, depression, and guilt, God steps into their human weakness and lifts them out of the depths of despair. That is how God works good into the lives of survivors of victimization. Jesus said, "I have told you these things, so that in me you may have peace. In this world you will have trouble. But take heart! I have overcome the world" (John 16:33).

God knew you would experience the sting of pain and suffering. With that understanding, He offers the encouraging words that He has "overcome the world." In the midst of your humanness, He can reach into your life and help you stand again. He brings peace to turmoil, order to chaos, and hope to despair. He wants to help you move beyond being a victim, to becoming a survivor. Truly He is a good God!

seven

Surviving the Betrayal of Childhood

THE CHILDHOOD VICTIM OF SEXUAL ABUSE IS CLEARLY AT A disadvantage, being at the mercy of a bigger, more powerful, and more intellectually advanced adult. From an early age children trust adults to love and nurture them in healthy, positive ways. However, in sexual-abuse cases adults often put their own perceived needs before their child and create perverted expressions of affection, which have devastating effects on the child.

Many victims experience tremendous guilt over their abuse. Cathleen felt the incestuous relationship with Dad was her fault, because she never told anyone. Martha described her guilt and confusion another way: "My offender started molesting me when I was twelve and the whole ordeal went on four years. I hated the control he had over me, but part of me enjoyed the closeness and sexual climax. I can't believe I actually found pleasure in that whole mess. A guilty confusion had me all tied up in knots!"

As we worked together in therapy, both Cathleen and Martha learned that they carried a weighty burden of false guilt. Letting go of it wasn't easy. Years of pain forged a thought pattern that flashed NAUGHTY GIRL! at every turn. Left with the task of making sense out of a senseless crime, their inexperienced youthfulness led them to very wrong conclusions.

In time, Cathleen understood why she could not tell anyone about her father. Martha learned that women are created with God-given desires for sexual pleasure. It was absolutely normal for her to enjoy sexual climax. With new insight, both women gradually began to unload their excess baggage of false guilt.

Common Problems

Many victims like Martha and Cathleen struggle not only with guilt but with strained interpersonal relationships.[1] Molestation contributes to the impairment of children's people-relating abilities in three vital areas:

1. Their willingness to trust

2. Their sense of protection

3. Their desire to socially relate with others

I Can't Trust Anybody!

Many victims struggle with an inability to trust.[2] Past betrayal by those they deeply loved makes it very hard for them to place confidence in God, husbands, family, or friends. In order to guard themselves from further wounds, victims erect walls around themselves. They tend to be extremely fearful and never fully trust what others say or do. Marriages, family ties, friendships, and work relationships often suffer the destructive aftermath of this violation of trust.[3]

Marian suffered sexual betrayal as a child and felt virtually powerless in adulthood. To combat the anxiety this image produced, she vowed to trust no one, because trust demanded vulnerability. While protecting herself from future victimization, she also wreaked havoc in most of her relationships.

After several months of therapy, Marian began to rebuild trust in others. As she grew in her relationship with God she experienced His ability to satisfy her deepest needs for love, security, and belonging. When she allowed Him to fill the voids from her past, she could effectively release others from her expectations.

Marian took practical steps to develop trust. First, she asked God to help her depend on Him as her primary source of love and acceptance. Since her father abused her for so many years, she found it very difficult to picture God as a loving heavenly Father. A Bible study on God's perfect character helped her move beyond old faulty perceptions to establish a new view of God as He really is.

During one assignment Marian wrote down every characteristic she recalled that described her earthly father. On the other side of the page, from her Bible studies, she listed all the characteristics of her heavenly Father. She forced herself to make a clean, precise distinction between the dad of her past, and the *Abba* ("Daddy") Father of her present (Romans 8:15 NAS).

In the process Marian grew to know God in a beautiful new way. Here are some of her thoughts:

God is

A Father to the Fatherless. God, You see my trouble and grief. You seriously consider my pain. As I commit myself to You, You promise to be a Father to me . . . a father of the fatherless (Psalms 10:14; 68:5).

Merciful. Thank You, God, for being a Father who is merciful (Luke 6:36).

Comforting. I praise You, God, because You are a Father of compassion and the God of all comfort (2 Corinthians 1:3).

Faithful. Thank You, God, that You are a faithful God who promises to love me and my children and all those who love You and who keep Your commands (Deuteronomy 7:9).

Kind. God, I praise You for setting a good example for me. You are kind, even to those who are ungrateful and wicked (Luke 6:35).

Loving. Thank You, God, for loving me so much. No one else can top Your love, because You died for me (John 15:13).

Just. Father, I praise You because righteousness and justice are the foundation of Your throne; love and faithfulness are at the core of Your character (Psalms 89:14).

Good. God, I'm so glad I'm Your child, because You only give good gifts to Your children (Psalms 85:12; Matthew 7:11).

Compassionate. Thank You, Father, that Your compassions never fail. They are new every morning (Lamentations 3:22, 23).

Protective. God, You have helped me by giving me strength. As I trust You for protection I feel a great sense of relief (Psalms 28:7).

Perfect. Lord, Your way is perfect, and Your Word is flawless (Psalms 18:30).

In addition to developing a more accurate perspective of God, Marian also asked God for courage to reach out to others. She had been accustomed to working all day in a closed office and hibernating at night in front of the television. In order to break the isolation, she set small goals to involve herself with others. One week she made two phone calls to friends. The next week she asked an associate to eat lunch with her. After several months she ventured out of her home at night to attend church gatherings and her athletic club. Going to an aerobics class was a major breakthrough for her.

All these efforts were outside of Marian's comfort zone. At first trusting others seemed risky. But as time passed she learned that God was by her side to encourage and help. When friends disappointed her, she talked with Him about her sadness and tried not to overgeneralize people's failures. Just because one person let her down, that didn't mean everyone in the world had copped out on her.

We saw wonderful changes take place in Marian. As God showed her that He was dependable, Marian released others from unrealistic expectations and began experiencing joy and freedom in her relationships. She also marveled at God's love ministering to her through her friends.

No One Will Protect Me!

Children trust adults to guard them from harm. But when sexual abuse occurs, this does not happen, and adult survivors usually struggle with intense anger towards those they think had the ability to stop their molestation.[4] They may direct their anger at God, mothers, brothers, sisters, or friends. Victims feel violated not only by offenders, but also by the entire family system.

As an abused child, Georgene felt powerless at the hands of her offending father. She was consumed with anger towards her mother, for allowing the abuse. After three failed marriages, she sat in my office and cried: "I can't understand why Dan [her husband] doesn't defend me. He allows his father to walk all over me and doesn't say a word. He says I need to speak for myself, but I think it's the husband's place to protect his wife. I shouldn't have to put up with his father's curt remarks when Dan is with me!"

Through months of therapy, Georgene began to understand how she played the victim in her marriage and viewed Dan as her only source of rescue. She saw herself as helpless and needing protection from possible danger. When Dan didn't meet her unrealistic expectations for nurturing and defense, she felt he had failed her.

Since victims were not protected as children, they usually look for nurturing friends who will jump to their rescue in adulthood. If they perceive that others do not carefully shelter them, they feel violated all over again. This hyper-dependency places considerable strain on interpersonal relationships. Sooner or later, victims wear out their friends with unrealistic demands.

In order to break the paralysis these unmet needs foster, many victims find it helpful to evaluate their parental relationships by asking themselves several important questions:

1. What did I need from Dad that I never received?

2. What did I need from Mom that I never received?

3. How am I attempting to meet these needs now?

4. Are my attempts to meet my needs appropriate?

5. Are there some better ways of meeting my needs?

In evaluating your past and present relationships, you may find it helpful to consider the areas illustrated in Chart 5.

I'm Uncomfortable Around Other People

Earlier we mentioned that offenders aggressively cut off their victims from outside help.[5] Since abuse usually occurs for years, isolated victims rarely learn good social skills and effective ways of relating with others.[6] Offenders have brainwashed them to believe that life outside the home is harmful and scary. When others do care for them, victims have a hard time recognizing it.

Ginger was in therapy for over a year before she believed I genuinely cared for her. When she discovered her inability to manipulate me, in anger she gave me the silent treatment. After a few weeks, the truth came out, when she blurted, "You don't really care about me or my feelings! If you did, you would have called or come over when I didn't keep my appointments." In time, Ginger realized that someone who genuinely cares does not reinforce manipulative and unhealthy behavior.

Ginger also learned to be sensitive to others and worked at not being self-absorbed. In group therapy one afternoon she explained her progress: "I've learned that my feelings are valid and worth sharing, but I need to make sure I don't violate or hurt someone else when I express them. The best way I can reveal my feelings without offending loved ones is by talking about my

Chart 5

What I wish I received from Mom or Dad, but didn't	How am I meeting this need now?	Healthy options (If needed)
MOM		
Mollie felt her mother never cared to understand her.	At twenty-two years of age, Mollie tried to explain herself and her actions to everyone, like a little girl wishing to be believed and understood.	Mollie learned through therapy that she did not have to explain herself to everyone. It was unrealistic to believe that everyone would always understand.
Diane's mother did not protect her from her father's sexual violations.	Feeling powerless, Diane did not defend herself in tight spots and relied totally on her husband for rescue.	Diane began to realize that she had more power as an adult than as a child. It was not fair or reasonable to expect her husband to bail her out of every conflict. She had resources to assist herself.
DAD		
Jean felt her father gave her sex instead of love.	Jean enjoyed emotional closeness with her husband, but avoided sex with him because it reminded her of her father.	Jean aggressively focused on the fact that her husband was not her father. She also took steps to act on this distinction, regardless of her feelings. During marital counseling, on a weekly basis, she and her husband set small, specific goals for their sexual relationship.

needs, instead of acting them out like a frustrated little kid. This has relieved a lot of strain in my relationships.

"I used to walk out on my friends, pout, and give them the silent treatment whenever they made me mad. But not anymore. I've learned that no one has the power to make me mad. I can be angry if I make that choice, but my feelings are my responsibility. Now my friends know where I stand. We don't play guessing games anymore. Since I've learned to trust in God's love, I don't have to cling to people as my only source of acceptance and companionship."

Ginger also evaluated the size and intensity of her needs. She recognized her overwhelming sense of dependency on her boyfriend. Whenever he didn't call precisely on time, she panicked. With thoughts racing viciously through her mind, she convinced herself he didn't love her anymore and was going to dump the relationship. She ruminated on ideas like *I'm not good enough. He's probably out with another girl who is skinny and prettier than me. I'm going to be an old maid, and no one will ever want to marry me.* Her entire life revolved around his every move.

In evaluating her needs, Ginger found it helpful to ask herself these questions:

1. Is there one area in my life that feels completely out of balance?

2. Does one particular need seem out of proportion to the rest?

3. Do I have a void in my life that seems completely unbearable?

Perhaps you can use these questions to study the size and intensity of your needs, too.

If these questions trigger a yes response, chances are your perceived needs are great. Several positive results can occur from this kind of evaluation. First, you can begin to understand and nurture the abused child of your past. We encourage victims to deliberately choose to quit being hard on the little girl they used to be. You may have to forgive yourself for being powerless and release yourself from the unrealistic expectation of holding your family together.

In order to nurture the abused child of your past, stop judging her for the responses she made. She was a scared little girl in a powerless, no-win situation. Anyone in her shoes would have done the same thing! Make friends with her. Accept the fact that her feelings were legitimate. As an adult, comfort that frightened little girl. Be strong for her. You are not powerless now.

By understanding your natural tendencies to overreact in certain situations you can better monitor your responses. This helps prevent foot-in-mouth syndrome and guards you from splattering others all over the pavement when they cross you.

A wise man once said, "No problem can be changed until it's faced." But once you face it, you can change it. By acknowledging and evaluating the voids in your life, you'll be in a better position to allow God and others to meet your needs in appropriate ways.

From Generation to Generation

Victims from triangulated families tend to carry learned coping styles from childhood into their adult homes.[7] While we usually see this pattern, we want to emphasize that offenses are not automatically repeated when victims become parents.

Recently, at a large pastors' conference, I spoke on the problems of sexual abuse. A beautiful dark-haired woman approached me after the meeting and said, "I've heard that abuse is usually perpetuated from one generation to the next."

Her bright blue eyes quickly filled with tears. As I waited, in a broken voice she continued, "I was molested by my dad for over four years when I was young. My husband and I love our three daughters more than anything else in the world. I don't know what I'd do if they were ever abused."

In the next few moments I learned that she and her husband pastored a church in the Northwest and had recently encountered some sex-abuse cases in their congregation. That couple desperately wanted to know how to counsel victims and their families, and they needed tools to help offenders.

It was a joy to tell this woman that not all victims repeat abuse with their children. Since she and her husband had given their lives to serve God and hungered to learn about helping those in need, the likelihood of abuse happening in their home was minimal.

Education provides one of the greatest ways to prevent abuse. As Proverbs 24:5 (NAS) says, "A wise man is strong, And a man of knowledge increases power." The more this couple learned about victims, offenders, and the family dynamics involved in abuse, the more power they had to effectively minister. As they educated their own children to deal with inappropriate sexual advances, they protected them from harm. This couple felt determined not to become another negative statistic. With God's help and wise counsel, they are breaking the pattern between generations.

*   *   *

Learning about the dynamics of sexually dysfunctional families may have been an eye-opener for you; it was for Ginger. However, she began to understand her family relationships and made peace with her painful past. As she gained insight about her needs for nurturance, protection, and trust she understood why her relationships were often strained.

Therapy felt uncomfortable for Ginger, but as she persisted with it, fabulous changes happened in her life: "I realize now that the abused little girl of my past cries out for protection. I've learned that I am an adult woman now, and no one can take advantage of me unless I let him. I am in control, not my dad, my mom, or my friends. With the Lord confirming my worth as His child, I can say no to self-destructive things.

"At one time in my life I took drugs, slept around, and abused alcohol, because I wanted others to accept me. What I really needed to feel was God's acceptance. I didn't think He loved me, because of my past.

"Now I know that God cares for me as His own child. He knows me inside and out. In spite of my ugly parts, Jesus gave His life on the cross so that I could have a relationship with my Creator. God has convinced me of His acceptance and has taught me to love myself and others in fresh new ways. I don't have to be down on myself anymore. God has made me a new person."

Ginger chose to act on what she learned about self-respect, through making wise decisions. She decided not to destroy herself with drugs or sexual affairs. Instead she focused on her value as a child created in the image of God. This made it hard for others to manipulate, take advantage, or victimize her. Her actions told the world, "I matter to me, and with God on my side, I can take care of myself."

As Ginger received God's unconditional acceptance and trusted

His ability to heal her deep wounds she and God worked together in partnership towards her wholeness. Today she is a brilliant example of a victim who has moved beyond the bondage of abuse. "Indeed, if any woman is in Christ, she is a new creature; the old things passed away; behold, new things have come" (*see* 2 Corinthians 5:17).

part four

MOVING
BEYOND
VICTIMIZATION

eight

Giving Yourself the Right to Grieve

E LLEN WAS FIRST TO SHARE WITH THE SUPPORT GROUP ONE night. With a bit of confusion, she described some of her feelings during the previous week: "It was strange. For some reason I started thinking about earlier years, and my childhood losses appeared in vivid pictures in my mind. I realized that almost overnight I changed from a carefree, innocent little girl to a fearful and burdened little adult. My childhood was robbed. I was forced to grow up too soon. . . . I wish I could go back and make things different."

Ellen's recognition of her childhood losses was a significant turning point in her healing process. When she openly acknowledged her grief, she received support from other members in the group, which helped buffer her depression.

Stages of Grief

Studies estimate that 85 percent of the time depression is caused by the loss of something significant in our lives.[1] While psychologists do not classify grief reactions to loss as clinical depression, depression *can* result when a person gets "stuck" in the grief process.

The normal grief process contains five progressive stages[2]:

1. Denial

2. Anger turned outward

3. Anger turned inward

4. Genuine sorrow

5. Resolution and acceptance

Research and experience show that victims of sexual abuse often get hung up in one stage. However, as they clear away roadblocks and progress through the five stages of grief, they experience recovery. In the following pages you'll meet some people who found themselves caught in one step. As you read their stories, be encouraged! They didn't stay stuck forever.

Stage 1: Denial

Denial is in operation when a person refuses to perceive or admit to the existence of something, in order to protect himself from unpleasant aspects of reality.[3] When we deny, we shut disturbing thoughts out of our awareness.[4] Though denial temporarily reduces or prevents anxiety from surfacing, in the long run it produces harmful results.

Some victims, like Debbie, don't realize why they feel depressed, because they don't acknowledge their negative feelings. During our first counseling appointment, Debbie said: "I'm not sure why I came in for counseling. I have a good life and a wonderful husband. But I keep having nightmares about my childhood. My dad molested me when I was growing up, but I don't think of myself as a victim. It just happened, that's all. These nightmares bother me, though, because I've got three children and have to get my sleep!"

Debbie had practiced denial for so many years that she had insulated herself from her feelings. All she knew was that a heavy gray cloud seemed to hang over her, night and day. Her depression and nightmares indicated an unresolved loss in her life, yet she had developed such a sophisticated denial system that she couldn't connect her past abuse with her current unpleasant feelings.

Victims often practice denial in other ways. For example, they may ignore their offender, mother, or family and deny the importance of keeping these lost relationships. Others practice denial by losing themselves in a frenzied, nonstop daily routine. Workaholism, incessant talking, and hyper–busyness prevent them from getting in touch with themselves. Still a third group denies the reality of their pain by using drugs or alcohol.

By the time she came in for therapy, Cynthia had perfected some of these techniques. One morning she talked about her mother: "I say good riddance to her. What did *she* ever do for me? She let that old sleaze bag of a husband of hers paw me all the time. I'm glad she doesn't want anything to do with me. She did me a favor by kicking me out in the street. It's her problem if she doesn't have a daughter anymore. I don't care if I ever see her again!''

While Cynthia was great at telling herself she didn't care about her mother, others weren't as easily convinced. Her friends saw through her rough exterior and encouraged her to come in for help. Herein lies one key aspect of denial: When we deny, the only person we usually fool is ourselves!

Stage 2: Anger Turned Outward

This stage of grieving targets anger at those surrounding the abuse. Many victims feel angry at others for allowing the loss of their virginity; they feel robbed of childhood innocence.

Many victims don't feel secure expressing negative emotions directly. They usually dump their buckets of anger indirectly and inappropriately. Since loved ones are available, they generally become "safe" targets and receive the brunt of the victim's passive-aggressive behaviors. Seemingly innocent and unprovoking situations can trigger a rage of anger, built up over the years. A victim needs to learn to investigate whether a specific situation triggers her anger or whether it was merely the last straw laid on the back of an already overloaded camel!

Anger turned outward can be expressed appropriately. In chapter 7 we discussed a variety of ways to manage anger. Controlled expressions of negative emotion can help you successfully move through stage two and on to stage three of the grief process.

Unfortunately many victims short-circuit stage two and move straight to stage three. Rather than dealing with their anger towards others, they turn their anger inward and blame themselves. Ginny was full of bitterness over her abuse, but denied feeling angry towards those who wronged her, saying: "It was my fault. You always get what you deserve. If I hadn't been home alone, my uncle probably would have left me alone. It's my problem.''

Eventually Ginny realized that abuse does not occur in a vacuum. Once she admitted her anger and used some of the management exercises we mentioned earlier, she saw that she had not participated in the incest alone. Everything wasn't her fault. She had very little control over her situation, and her uncle should have known better. In time Ginny could say, "I've been wrong to carry the painful rap all these years. He robbed me of my virginity, my innocence, and my trust. *He* is to blame!'' After dealing with anger towards her uncle and others, Ginny began to manage the anger she had turned inward.

Stage 3: Anger Turned Inward

At some point during grief, victims usually turn their anger inward. Some feel angry at themselves for not getting help sooner, for not stopping the abuse, or for remaining silent so many years. Usually feelings of anger directed inward are coupled with intense feelings of true or false guilt. Care givers can do victims a favor by clarifying the difference between these two forms of guilt.

True guilt, the uncomfortable inner awareness that we have chosen to violate God's moral law, is produced partly by the conviction of God's Holy Spirit and partly by our own consciences.[5] Because it is God's way of getting our attention so that we will attend to a situation and do the right thing, this type of guilt has value. If a victim willfully seduced her father, she probably suffers true guilt.

While the conviction of the Holy Spirit initiates true guilt, *false guilt* arises out of an intense desire to please others. For example, if a victim feels insecure in her abilities to be all things to all people, she probably suffers from self-imposed false guilt. Since incest is a taboo, she may also feel guilty for having experienced a sexual relationship that deviates from society's expectations of normalcy. Christian psychiatrist Paul Tournier describes true and false guilt this way:

> *A feeling of* false guilt *results from social suggestion, fear of taboos or of losing the love of others. (Victims feel false guilt when they mistakenly believe they caused their own abuse.) However, a feeling of* true guilt *is the genuine consciousness of having betrayed an authentic standard; it is a free judgment of the self by the self. On this assumption, there is a complete opposition between these two guilt-producing mechanisms, the one acting by social suggestion, the other by moral conviction. . . .*
>
> *False guilt is that which comes as a result of the judgments and suggestions of men. (When offenders and/or mothers blame children for abuse, feelings of false guilt are set in motion.) True guilt is that which results from divine judgment. . . . Therefore true guilt is often something quite different from that which constantly weighs us down, because of our fear of social judgment and the disapproval of men.*[6]

In this third stage of grief, victims often become engulfed in a mire of self-imposed false guilt. They may feel guilty because they enjoyed the special attention and did not stop the molestation or because they didn't tell anyone about their abuse.

During therapy, Becky examined the difference between true and false guilt. Later in the healing process, she evaluated her feelings and penned these words in her journal:

I'm beginning to see how I blamed myself for my abuse. . . . It was easier to accept the fact that this was false guilt when I realized the responsibility for my abuse lies with my offender. I don't have to be angry at myself any longer. Perhaps I could have stopped my dad by telling Mom. I don't know. I will never know.

But even though I can't change my past, I can make the best of today and tomorrow. Knowing this makes me feel better.

Successfully processing anger turned inward is a strategic part of the healing process and a necessary prerequisite for moving forward and experiencing genuine sorrow over past losses.

Stage 4: Genuine Sorrow

When victims have moved through the first three stages, the realization of their losses becomes apparent, and genuine sorrow sets in. Tears sometimes flow uncontrollably, and sadness can seem overwhelming. If you are in this stage of grief, don't despair. It's okay to cry! God made your tear ducts for a reason, and crying is a healthy way of releasing the emotional energy inside you.

Some people describe genuine sorrow as acute psychological pain. In this stage victims experience often intense mood swings, emotional upheaval, and feelings of hurt, guilt, depression, anger, and loneliness. Many grievers feel disorganized and may wonder if they are losing their minds.[7] Sleep disturbances, appetite loss, and relationship conflicts may also occur.

During acute times of sorrow, victims also experience a deep yearning for things to return to the way they had been before the abuse. Fantasies, daydreaming, and wishes for a different ending to their story prevail, along with a desperation to retrieve what was lost.

In group therapy one evening, Patricia shared feelings typical of this stage: "I'm preoccupied with flashbacks of everything I lost during my abuse. It's as if I'm floundering in a sea of anxiety.

"I feel constantly on edge, and the tiniest things agitate me. When Steve takes Jenny to school, on his way to work, I get real phobic. It's as if I want to be with them every minute of the day, to make sure they aren't taken away from me, too.

"My nerves are raw. At times sadness and shame overwhelm me. I just don't know what to do with myself. Maybe this is what it feels like to lose your mind!"

Though genuine sorrow is emotionally draining and psychologically painful, it is a healthy response to loss. Without the expression of genuine sorrow, complete emotional recovery is not possible.[8]

When Patricia first came into therapy, she had her emotions tightly locked inside. She hadn't cried for years and didn't know what sadness felt like anymore. As time passed she gave herself permission to think about her losses, told herself she had a right to grieve, and allowed the tears to flow.

One afternoon she said, "I've spent a lot of time over the years fantasizing about what might have been. But fantasy isn't reality. I realize now that my fairy tales aren't going to magically materialize. It's hard, and it hurts to think about everything I've lost. But I have to face the facts and quit living in dreamland."

Recording her losses helped Patricia make strides through stage 4. She noted each loss on a three-by-five card and marked the date she accepted the reality of the loss. Her card looked something like this:

*1. I accepted losing my dad as a real
father on*   *January 2, 1985*

*2. I accepted losing my mother as a
protector on*   *January 5, 1985*

*3. I accepted the loss of my family as
a place where I felt I belonged on*   *January 6, 1985*

*4. I accepted the loss of my child-
hood innocence on*   *January 10, 1985*

Patricia also used a guided imagery exercise to help her visualize her progress as she accepted each loss. One day in therapy, from her journal she read a description of the pictures she used to give her hope during times of sorrow:

"I see myself as a castle on a hill. For a long time the castle was dark and covered with gloom. There were no lights in the windows. Scraggly bushes and weeds had overgrown its foundations. It looked as if it had been forgotten for years. As I accepted each loss, I imagined lights coming on in the windows of the castle.

"I have forgiven my father and mother for not being perfect parents. This has helped me not to expect perfection in myself or others. Since I never felt as if I belonged in my family, I made a promise to not let a day pass without telling my own children I was glad they were mine.

"Once I accepted that my childhood was gone forever, I became more content with life. When I made little steps of progress, I pictured more lights going on in my imaginary castle. My life is happier now, and joy comes more spontaneously. No more secrets darken my windows. The castle is ablaze with life and light!"

Grief has no painless shortcuts. "To get beyond grief, one

must go through it, not around it.'' For complete recovery to occur, we must experience genuine sorrow and release our emotions in ways that respect others. We must be willing to share our pain and let others give us comfort.[9]

Group therapy can be extremely helpful during grief. As victims experience genuine sorrow over their losses, others who know what it's like to walk a mile in their shoes surround them. As grieving victims allow themselves to receive support, roadblocks can be cleared, and they can move on to the final stage of grief.

Stage 5: Resolution and Acceptance

In most cases, victims automatically move on to resolution and acceptance, after working through the first four stages of grief.[10] Resolution is characterized by a realistic acknowledgment and acceptance of losses. At this point, a person feels willing to pick up the pieces of life and move forward. Note the word *willing*. If a victim does not want to go on with life, she has not adequately worked through the first four stages.

As the victim acknowledges and accepts losses a strong survivor emerges. ''It's as if the victim says, 'The worst possible thing that could happen did happen. And I survived it. Now, I'm ready to get on with life.' ''[11] At this time decreased irritability becomes apparent, and the survivor seems better able to understand herself. She becomes more autonomous, sensitive to others, and better able to form friendships. Her ability to enjoy life increases, and she lives in the present and future, rather than the past.

Processing the five stages of grief doesn't happen in five hours or five days. It takes time. Research shows that a person rarely resolves grief in less than one year to eighteen months after a loss is perceived.[12] Be patient with yourself, and in the meantime look for glimpses of hope in your grief.

Finding Hope in the Grief Process

During the years following your sexual abuse, no doubt you have suffered many forms of disappointment. Disillusionment may have crept over you like a cloud, blocking out hope and happiness.

In the midst of your grief, however, you can experience points of relief. Here are some of the things that have helped ease other victims' burdens.

1. In the midst of your sorrow, recognize that things will get better. Eventually you will leave behind the miserable feelings and hopelessness. Extreme lows will not hang around you forever. One day you'll look back on all this. Focus on the parts of your life that have hope.

2. Recognize that grief is unavoidable and normal. It is a necessary process, the only healthy way to deal with loss. The length of time you spend in each stage of grief may vary considerably, depending on the extent of your isolation, family support, belief in God, and so on.

Just when you feel acceptance settling in, you may battle with another outburst of despair. Understand that unpleasant, painful emotions will come and go—sometimes in a flood, sometimes in a trickle. Realize that the change of moods you're experiencing is natural and appropriate.

After the death of his wife, C. S. Lewis commented:

Grief is like a long and winding valley where any bend may reveal a totally new landscape. . . . Sometimes the surprise is the opposite one; you are presented with exactly the same sort of country you thought you left behind miles ago. That is when you wonder whether the valley isn't a circular trench. But it isn't. There are partial recurrences but the sequence doesn't repeat.[13]

Expect fluctuating emotions. Sometimes your emotions will race in and out without any logical progression. You won't always keep up with them. At those times talk to yourself out loud. Remind your intellect that grief feelings are normal. You aren't unspiritual to feel them. You aren't going off the deep end. You are merely walking through the normal grieving process.

3. Realize that action is sometimes necessary for escape. You've heard the old saying, "It's easier to act yourself into a new way of thinking than to think yourself into a new way of acting." This sounds simplistic, but it works.

What do you like to do outside your home? What projects have you wanted to tackle around the house? This is a time to indulge yourself! Do what you like to do. Plan some special things to look forward to. Schedule some time to tackle those "need to do's" around the house. Capitalize on your emotional energy and make it work for you, rather than allowing it to work against you.

One word of caution. Many victims go overboard indulging in food. Bulimia and other related eating disorders are found in a high percentage of abuse cases. In an effort to fill voids in their lives or to escape from pain, many victims become entrapped in the binge-purge cycle. This only complicates matters and drives them deeper into depression. Food won't satisfy the cravings of the soul. But there is Someone who will.

Your disappointments can be a catalyst for a renewed dependence on God. In your feeling of hopelessness, you can turn to the ultimate Source of encouragement and hope. He will show Himself strong on your behalf!

When disappointment exploded in Karen's heart, she longed for things to be as they were before her abuse. No human being could diminish her hurt. Only God could offer her comfort during those private times of sorrow.

Karen's pain brought about significant growth in her life, deepening her dependence on and communion with God. She learned what it felt like to see no physical cure for her wounds. Although family and friends helped to a degree, only God really knew when she suffered in silence.

Many victims like Karen become strong survivors once they allow themselves the right to grieve. If you are experiencing despair, remember this is a normal reaction to your loss. Allow God to intercept you at your deepest points of sorrow. Trying to walk the road ahead alone will deprive you of a great experience with God. As you turn to Him in your weakness He will channel hope into your desert of despair. He will begin a new work in you!

It may not happen all at once. This new work will probably come in bits and pieces, through circumstances and individuals God puts in your life, through communion and sharing with Him. Remember, as a child of God, you are in process. Even when you don't feel His presence, God continues to be your Father. You are His continual "workmanship" (Ephesians 2:10) and His piece of art. He will continue healing. He has not left you. He is at work in you today.

nine

Airing the Wounds

THE NEXT TWO CHAPTERS WILL OFFER YOU SOME LIFE BUOYS to guide you as you sail across the stormy waters of victimization to the stable shores of survivorhood. Use the practical suggestions here to learn to appropriately express your feelings.

Facing Your Emotions

As you seek healing from your abuse, air your wounds in your emotional life. One of the worst things you can do—both for yourself and for those around you—is to keep negative emotions bottled inside. By pretending bad feelings don't exist, you only prolong the agony.

Instead of packing away those emotions, use *ventilation, assimilation,* and *confrontation* to shed your burden of concealed hurt.[1]

Ventilation

A home constructed with good ventilation allows fresh air currents to reach all the rooms, keeping air inside clean and purified. If the vent system breaks down, air stagnates, mold appears, and bad odors accumulate.

When we use the term *ventilate* in counseling, we mean a close examination and open discussion of something, for the purpose of cleansing. Most victims struggle with negative emotions. Often they express anger, the most prominent of their uncomfortable feelings; but stuffed anger usually comes out in unpredictable and destructive ways. Just as a good venting system keeps air from stagnating in a home, emotional ventilation can help victims manage their anger and cleanse their hearts of negative feelings.

It's Okay to Feel Angry!

Some Christians mistakenly believe all anger is wrong and ungodly. However, a close look at Scripture shows us verses like Ephesians 4:26, which tells us "In your anger do not sin: Do not let the sun go down while you are still angry."

In the English New Testament, several Greek words have been translated "anger." The one in Ephesians 4:26, *orge,* means "intense anger that comes as a reaction against sin or injustice"— a far cry from our usual understanding of our English word.

God endorses anger against injustice and sin. However, He also commands that in our anger we must remain in control and "not sin." H. Norman Wright explains the ingredients of righteous anger.

The word angry *[in Ephesians 4:26] means an anger which is an abiding and settled habit of the mind, and which is aroused under certain conditions. The person is aware and in control of it. There is a just occasion for the anger here. Reason is involved and when reason is present anger such as this is right.*[2]

If you feel angry about your abuse, your emotions are justified. Your offender was wrong! He ripped you off. Your circumstances were not fair. You know it, we know it, and God knows it. So give yourself permission to feel angry. Don't stuff those negative feelings into a corner and allow them to fester into a cancerous bitterness.

On the positive side, anger may serve as a cue to tell you that the time has come for you to begin to cope and deal with your inner feelings. As anger begins to build, focus your attention on that surging energy. Ask yourself, *What am I feeling right now? Why am I feeling this way?* Tune in to those signals of anger. They can help you work through your grief.

Expressing Anger

Many of us fail to distinguish between having a feeling, expressing a feeling, and acting on a feeling. Like many victims, you may need to be encouraged to take the crucial step of identifying the emotion of anger and saying, "I feel angry." When you admit to feelings of anger, you have not sinned, but taken a step in the right direction. Stuffing anger away is like holding a hot coal in your hand. *You* get burned.

After you have identified and admitted your anger, express it. But remember: Anger is powerful; it can be extremely destructive or constructive. The result depends upon the manner of expression. Kicking, swearing, screaming and throwing yourself into fits of rage all express anger. But you may find the results they bring less than rewarding!

You have better options. Some people find it helpful to jog or do some type of aerobic exercise. Other women aggressively attack their kitchen floors with scrub brushes and their cupboards with sponges. Try digging in the garden or running around the block.

It also helps to write your feelings in a journal, talk into a tape recorder, or tell your concerns to a trusted friend.

Letters as a Safety Valve

Some victims write letters in order to express their anger without hurting others. Usually they don't send these letters, but this type of ventilation can bring relief. As they write they describe the fear, guilt, anger, and betrayal they felt as a victimized, unprotected child. One benefit of writing is that the paper and ink can't talk back.

One woman expressed her feelings towards her offender in this letter:

Dear Dad:

Please read this letter with an open heart, it is written from my heart and is not meant to hurt or attack you.

I need to tell you how I felt the seven years you sexually assaulted me. It is very hard for me to write this, and my whole body is trembling with fear and anger.

Fear is what I remember as I think of being six years old. Oh God why. . . . I remember the first time you raped me. You took me on a business trip with you. I was so excited, just me and my Daddy and getting to stay in a motel and eating out in restaurants with you.

It wasn't until that evening that my childhood crumbled. I remember you taking my clothes off and how trusting I was; even as you told me that what you were going to do was something wonderful, and that all little girls love it. Then came the tearing pain. I remember you covering my mouth to stifle my screams and the whole time telling me next time it won't hurt so much. I prayed . . . God please don't let him do this to me again. But God didn't hear my prayers and I prayed for his mercy every day for seven years. I hated you that night and I continued to hate and fear you for years. I remember when you had finished, I was still crying, and to this day I remember the pain I felt that night. You then asked me if I loved my mommie and I said yes. You asked if I loved my sisters and brothers and I said yes. That's when you told me if I told anyone of what you did to me you would put mom and everyone else against a wall and shoot them one by one and it would be my fault because I didn't keep your secret. I kept the secret and you found other ways to make sure I didn't tell as I got older remember . . .

For the next two years I only remember feeling confused

and terrified of being alone with you and wondering when it would happen again.

Then I turned eight, I felt a hundred and wished I was dead. I remember thinking I couldn't experience anything else that could make me feel more hurt than I already felt in my heart. Until the night you decided to force me to have oral sex with you. I remember you pinning my head down and the gagging and choking (it seemed as though you pinned me for an eternity) and how much I wanted to throw up. But even more important, I remember not being able to eat without choking and gagging because of flash backs. For years Dad I couldn't stand to have anyone touch the back of my neck because of the tremendous force you used on me then and in the following years. Then came the night you fed me booze and I remember crying and feeling sick from the liquor and the fear of knowing something awful was going to happen. Then my fear became a reality and you forced anal sex. I remember screaming out in pain and you hitting me and telling me to shut up. I thought I was ripping apart and my only thoughts were prayers to God as I remembered the pain I had felt at age six and asked God when it would end.

I could go on and on about incidents. I've only made you remember three out of hundreds. And now to the reason why I'm writing. I have just found out that you are doing these same things to your stepdaughter. The anger I kept hidden for years because of you erupted when I learned that you are still hurting children. I want you to realize that Annie trusted you once and loved you more than anyone and she could again, if you give her a father she can trust and love. If not, then you and only you will have to learn to live

*with the memories of her screams of pain and my screams
of pain. Please look inside of yourself and try to seek help.
I beg you, please spare Annie the nights I cried myself to
sleep, the memories of nightmares and the years of wanting
to run or die. Most of all please give her back the father she
trusted and loved.*

© 1979

Rape and Abuse Crisis Center
"All Rights Reserved"

(This letter was submitted by the Rape Abuse Crisis Center in Fargo,
North Dakota. It was written by an incest victim who is now a
professional working with victims of sexual abuse.)

As you read this letter, perhaps you identified with every line
and admired the courage of this young woman who faced her
offender. At the same time, you may have thought, *I don't think
I'll ever be able to tell my offender exactly how I feel!* Confrontation seems an insurmountable task, because of bitter anger
smouldering within. In chapter 10, we will talk about how to
confront an offender. But before this can successfully occur,
you'll need to face and manage your anger.

Letters for other family members. Since many victims have
strong feelings towards the mother or loved ones who didn't
protect them, it can be therapeutic to repeat the previous exercise
with these people in mind. During one of our evening sessions,
Sandra shared a letter she had written to her mother, asking
questions she had longed to have answered for years:

Dear Mom:

*I don't know where to begin. Most of the time I feel we're
strangers. I don't know how you'll receive what I'm about*

to say. I tried to talk to you about this many times, but it always seemed you weren't interested. One time I did tell you about Dad, but you didn't believe me and told me to never mention it again. Since that time I felt you didn't believe anything I said.

I'm in therapy now and realize that my thoughts and feelings are important. That's why I need to tell you how I felt when you closed me out and didn't listen.

Mom, I was abused and exploited by Dad. Do you know what it's like to have your father ask for sexual favors when you're only nine years old? He told me you couldn't have sex with him, because you were sick, and I needed to take your place. I believed him.

Didn't you ever wonder where he was early in the morning, or why he took so long to get me up to go to school? Did you ever ask him? I don't think you ever noticed what was happening. Everything was okay as long as we didn't bother you. That was pretending, Mom, not reality.

The reality is that Dad sexually molested Tanya and me for nine years. My abuse finally ended when I left for college. I felt betrayed by both you and Dad. Dad molested me, but you allowed it, without saying a word. I am very angry, Mom, because you did nothing! I depended on you, and you let me down. I also feel upset because you refused to listen to me and to acknowledge ten years of my life.

Sandra cried softly as she finished reading her letter.

"How does it feel to confront your mother with your feelings?" I asked.

After a long pause, she replied, "The big lump in my throat is gone. I've wanted to tell my mother this for years. It feels good to get it out. It may not change things with Mom, but at least *I* feel relief.''

Another victim, Melanie, struggled with a different problem. Her older brother, Jack, continuously turned his back when his high-school buddy molested Melanie. Six years later Melanie wrote this letter:

Dear Jack:

There's a question I've wanted to ask you but haven't because I was afraid of how you might answer. You knew Marty molested me all those years, didn't you? How many times did you walk in on us and then sheepishly back out the door? I remember pleading with you for help. Why, Jack? Why didn't you stop it or at least tell someone what was going on? I was your sister!

I feel betrayed by your silence. I was much younger and looked to you for protection. You let Marty do whatever he wanted to me so he would be your friend. I am angry that you allowed him to exploit me.

Maybe if you weren't my brother, it wouldn't hurt so badly. I loved you and looked up to you. I feel as if you failed me when I needed you most.

> *Wanting an answer,*
> *Melanie*

Although letters like Sandra's and Melanie's are usually not mailed, some people do send their feelings in writing to the individuals surrounding their abuse. Unfortunately, the victims may also erroneously base the success of their expressions on the reactions they receive from their offenders, mothers, or loved ones. Remember, the value of these communications is not contained in a reply.

You can't control other people's responses. Those who surround your abuse are responsible for their feelings and actions. Although they may not answer your communications the way you would like, you can still benefit from honestly expressing your feelings.

Ventilation can help you lance this boil, remove the poison, and air the injury. Expressing swallowed pain has the primary purpose of helping you understand and take responsibility for your emotions. As you become aware of and use your powers to control your feelings, you can move away from bitterness, towards forgiveness and healing.

Letters to God. God is not intimidated by your anger or caught off guard by your frustration. He understands and loves you. Talk with Him and keep your lines of communication open. Even though He already knows every minute detail of your past, present, and future, talking with Him will help you gain perspective. The Bible says, "Come near to God and he will come near to you . . ." (James 4:8). As you take a step towards God, He will keep His promise and comfort you.

Some victims find it helpful to write letters to God. They tell Him exactly how they feel and honestly express their thoughts about their abuse. Kathi struggled with anger towards God and wrote Him this letter:

Dear God,

I've been taught that it's wrong to get angry with You, but I need to be honest. It's hard for me to tell You this, because I'm afraid, but I can't go on feeling this way. I've swallowed a lot of anger and resentment towards You because You allowed my abuse. Plus my father got off without a hitch. God, that isn't fair. At least it isn't in my book.

I want to believe You have heard me, Lord, and I want to get rid of this bitterness. Please understand my anger and pain. Please take away the ugly attitudes I have inside. Clean up my heart. I can't do it alone. Thank You for listening to me.

Love,

Kathi

More Ideas for Ventilating Feelings

The empty-chair exercise. Another way to ventilate bottled feelings is to use the empty chair exercise.[3] Sherilee found this extremely helpful. One afternoon, while home alone, she placed two chairs so they faced each other and sat in one. She imagined her offender sitting across from her and told him how she felt about all the years of abuse, unloading anger, disappointment, powerlessness, helplessness, fear, and all the other emotions she had experienced. Although Sherilee knew she didn't have the courage to see her offender in person, the exercise took her one step further in that direction.

Victims may also use the empty chair exercise to help work towards settling accounts with the others surrounding their abuse. One evening Elizabeth imagined her offending brother in the chair across from her and confronted him with these words:

John, I hated you for the years of torture you put me through. You always grabbed me when no one was looking. When Mom and Dad asked you to baby-sit me, you overstepped your bounds. I felt so helpless when you took advantage of me. You were so strong, there was no way I could have escaped. I loved you, and this was how you 'loved' me!

When I see Mom make a fuss over your successes, I want to vomit. I wish she knew what you were really like!

Of course, she wouldn't believe me, even if I told her. She said I was a liar when I told her you were sleeping with your boss in order to climb the corporate ladder. Oh yes, I told her. That was my way of getting back at you for what you did to me. But don't worry, she didn't believe me. She never did believe me. You were always an expert at giving her a good snow job. I hated the ways you got away with murder while I had to take the rap.

For thirteen years Elizabeth buried anger and resentment towards her brother deep inside. With the help of tools like the empty chair exercise and letter writing, she eventually managed her emotions and stabilized her mood swings. She also used the following technique, SIFE, in her recovery process.

SIFE. Another tool for constructively venting negative emotions, can be captured in the acronym SIFE.[4] As a victim evaluates life circumstances by using four specific steps, she is able to more easily handle intense emotions. The four steps, *Situation, Interpretation, Feeling* and *Expression* are explained below:

1. **Assess the *Situation:*** Take the important step of assessing each situation. Your perception of what goes on around you is very important. What do you see, hear, and

detect with your physical senses? What expectations do you have? Usually you perceive what you expect to perceive.

2. *Interpret* the Situation: When you interpret a situation, you place meaning and make judgments about your perceptions. Records of childhood memories are carried in your mind. You tend to interpret present-day situations the same way you did as a child. When "new" situations push "old" buttons, sometimes you can erroneously jump to your childhood conclusions. Adults need to learn to make new interpretations.

3. **Tune In to Your** *Feelings:* Feelings—learned reflexes to present, split-second interpretations—often impair your ability to accurately assess a situation. As you no longer deny feelings, but ventilate and express them, you set the stage for more objective and appropriate interpretations of present situations.

4. **Check Your** *Expression:* When you express your feelings, you behave in ways that represent what goes on inside your heart and mind. Emotions are manifested in your actions, either aggressively, through overt expression, or passively, through withdrawal and silence.

Chart 6 illustrates how emotionally charged situations can be processed using SIFE.

Some Final Thoughts About Ventilation

When we deal with negative emotions, it helps to remember that we live in a fallen world. Bumps and bruises are all a part of this lost system. Instead of falling for the irrational notion that a

Chart 6

Situation	Unhealthy Interpretation Based on Abused Past	Feeling	Expression
Maria's boss asked her to work late again, for the third time this week.	Maria thought her boss's requests were manipulative. She felt he was taking advantage of her, thinking she was a "pushover." Maria's past colored her present interpretation: Though she had said no continuously, Maria's abusive brother ignored her protests and forced himself on her. Deep down inside Maria thought she must be an easy mark because of this.	Rage	Maria didn't tell her boss how she felt. Instead, she ranted and raved to her husband for not feeding the dog. (Her anger was expressed, but dumped inappropriately on her spouse.)
Cathy and John were attracted to each other, and he asked her out on a date.	Cathy was sure John wanted more out of the relationship than she was ready to give. Cathy's present interpretation was colored by her past: All Cathy had wanted from	Fear	Cathy always made excuses not to go out. (Rather than dealing with her fears, Cathy withdrew and isolated herself from an enriching social life.

Chart 6 (Continued)

Situation	Unhealthy Interpretation Based on Abused Past	Feeling	Expression
	her dad was his attention and love. He gave her sex instead. She felt sure all men were the same.		

Situation	Healthy Interpretation	Feeling	Expression
Jennifer's husband, Bob, lectured her again, telling her to avoid her mother. Bob believed Jennifer shouldn't bring up the subject of her abuse with her mother.	Jennifer realized that Bob was trying to protect her from the pain of confrontation, instead of supporting her through it. (Jennifer stopped the old tape of never feeling heard and tried to understand what she communicated to Bob.)	Misunderstood	Jennifer told Bob of her need for him to listen. She also expressed her appreciation for his desire to protect her, but said she needed his quiet support even more.
Susie's friend violated her confidence by telling a mutual friend about Susie's abuse.	Susie wisely saw this as her friend's problem and stopped the old tape that her secrets were of no value to anyone.	Frustration	Susie planned in advance to lovingly confront her friend, using "I feel" statements.

Christian should never feel turmoil, we need to understand that we cannot live with ourselves or one another without experiencing unpleasant feelings from time to time.

Scripture gives further insight into managing our fires within. God says:

"Better a patient man than a warrior, a man who controls his temper than one who takes a city" (Proverbs 16:32). Controlling our emotions is better than allowing them to control us. When we lose control, matters often get worse.

"My dear brothers, take note of this: Everyone should be quick to listen, slow to speak and slow to become angry, for man's anger does not bring about the righteous life that God desires" (James 1:19, 20). These verses reveal an inherent choice for each one of us. We can choose to express negative emotions in constructive and appropriate ways, or we can try to live in fantasy land by denying the reality of our unpleasant feelings.

If you have suffered sexual abuse, anger is undoubtedly as much a part of your life as death and taxes; it is neither right nor wrong, it simply is. May we encourage you to handle your anger in appropriate ways? This will help speed up your recovery. As you use some of the tools that others have found bring relief you'll be on the road to managing your feelings, rather than letting them manage you.

ten

Getting the Big Picture

"WHEN I FIRST BEGAN THERAPY, I DIDN'T KNOW there were so many things to learn about sexual abuse," Rochelle said one afternoon. "I was aware of some of the pieces of the puzzle, but by no means saw the complete picture.

"Looking at incest through the eyes of other family members has broadened my perspectives. I realize now that my relationship with Dad held the family together in a perverted way. What happened to me was not just my problem. It was my mom and dad's problem, too.

"I used to just see film clips of my past in my mind. But now

I don't feel as if my childhood was as fragmented. The bigger picture has started to come into focus. Things seem to make more sense now, and I think I can leave the past behind.''

Research very clearly shows that incest is not an isolated event. Family dynamics play a primary role in the development and continuation of sexual abuse.[1] In many cases, it has been shown to actually hold families together.[2] The family stagnates in abuse because change (such as a parent leaving) is perceived as being traumatic.[3]

Given the opportunity to consider their abuse from the perspective of others, victims can find missing pieces of the puzzle. They can begin to see the bigger picture. Assimilating their past experience helps them understand what took place, so that closure of their trauma can occur.

Assimilation

The dictionary defines *assimilation* as the act of comparing, absorbing, and incorporating.[4] When we use the term in relation to sexual abuse, we refer to the victim's ability to grasp a variety of perspectives of her abuse. Assimilation occurs as victims compare and absorb different viewpoints and insights about their sexual abuse.

Some victims initially resist thinking about their abuse from their fathers' and mothers' viewpoints, fearing this exercise will force them to excuse the wrongs they suffered. Still other victims don't want to look at the full picture because for years they denied or justified their abuse, based on what other family members said. Since they feel uncomfortable thinking about their parents being wrong, they ignore the situation, rather than facing it. Neither of these sponsors healing.

This chapter includes some assimilation techniques that help victims hypothetically examine the perspectives offenders and others may have had about their molestation. When victims assimilate their abuse, they consider and interpret each significant family member's input. We offer these tools to help broaden your understanding of your past and to assist you towards a closure of your abuse.

A Series of Letters

Seeing the big picture can come through writing a series of letters. This enables you to understand the perspectives of others, even though you don't agree with their rationalizations.

Try this suggestion. After writing a letter to your offender, imagine how he might answer you. How would your father feel, opening and reading your letter? Try to experience his emotions and thoughts.

Next write yourself a return letter, pretending you are your offender. Put yourself in his shoes and try to respond as he would to the first letter you wrote him. Continue these letters back and forth until you have said everything you want to say.

Jamie brought in a series of letters she had written. Her first letter began:

Dear Dad:

> *I have to tell you how I feel. I remember all the times you molested me early in the morning before school. For years I felt guilty, humiliated, and powerless because you did this to me. Right now I feel scared even writing you, because I don't know how you will react. We never talked about it when I was growing up, but I'm sure you remember.*

Dad, I'm angry. I still hurt from being used by you. It makes me sad to think you really didn't love me. Now I know that dads who truly love their kids don't misuse them. That hurts most of all because I tried hard to be good so you and Mom would love me.

Your daughter,
Jamie

Jamie imagined her father's response to her letter:

Dear Jamie:

I don't know why you're so angry. Those things happened many years ago. We have a good relationship now, don't we? It really wasn't so bad, was it? Everything turned out okay, after all.

You probably imagined a whole lot more than really happened. There's no sense in telling any of this to your mother. After all, there's no use in upsetting her now. If it's any consolation to you, I felt bad about what happened. Those were hard times for me, and I guess I went too far. Let's just forget about it, okay?

Love,
Dad

Jamie was not satisfied with her dad's response and wrote another letter:

Dear Dad:

All these years, your silence contributed to my guilt. I have blamed myself for what happened. But I'm in therapy now and realize that when a child is molested, it is the adult's fault. Dad, it was your responsibility not to exploit me, but you did it anyway. Why, Dad? Why?

Jamie

Finally, Jamie imagined her father writing this letter back to her:

Dear Jamie:

You are right. I was wrong to take advantage of your innocence. I take full responsibility for what happened. It was never your fault. Please don't blame yourself. Let's get together and talk. Maybe we can salvage our relationship. I want to do what is best for you, now.

Love,
Dad

Jamie was fortunate. Later in therapy she confronted her father face-to-face, and he actually did take responsibility for his actions. After his apologies and many hours of therapy, Jamie and her dad gradually rebuilt their relationship.

Unfortunately, these exercises are as close as many victims come to confronting their offenders. Some offenders die, some disappear, and others never acknowledge the abuse. At first doing these exercises may seem futile, especially if your offender is dead. However, remember that one of your goals in the healing process is to assimilate a more complete understanding of your abuse; this does not require a response from your offender. Many victims find that when they understand the context of their trauma, they can better close that chapter in their lives and put it to rest.

The Empty-Chair Exercise: Part Two

Earlier we showed you how Sherilee and Elizabeth used the empty-chair exercise to talk to their offenders. Later in therapy they used this tool again to help them more fully understand the context of their abuse. This time they played both roles, offender and victim. They imagined what their offenders thought and felt and how they would respond to confrontation.

Because of the negative emotions they experienced during role playing, we used relaxation exercises to help them calm their anxieties. As they switched back and forth, posing questions to their offenders and answering as they would, we instructed them to become aware of their bodies. We asked questions like, "What physical sensations do you notice? Do you have a knot in your stomach or a lump in your throat? When did these sensations occur? What precipitated them? What were you thinking when these feelings became apparent?"

We encourage victims using this technique to stop periodically and allow themselves to acknowledge physical and emotional arousal. Once they have done this, they use the *quieting response* to calm their minds and bodies. A description of this simple relaxation technique is included in Appendix I.

Some victims find it helpful to imagine their offender as he looks and acts today, rather than the way he was when they were children. This seems to provide them with an older, more mature, and approachable image. Jamie pictured her offending father, looking the way he looks now, with gray hair, tired eyes, and more wrinkles, saying: "Most of my life has passed me by, and I've made a mess of it. . . . My wife and I live in the same house, but we are strangers. We haven't made real contact for years. The kids don't visit very often, and when they do, they spend all their time with their mom. When did my life start to go wrong?"

Jamie also used the empty-chair exercise and letters in her journal to help her deal with negative feelings towards her mom. Gradually her courage increased, and eventually she talked with her mother in person. After several months she finally asked the question that had haunted her for years: "Mom, if you suspected what Dad was doing, why didn't you stop him?"

Jamie's mother looked at her with sad eyes and told her that she had wanted to pretend it wasn't happening. She loved Jamie's father, but it hurt too much to think he preferred Jamie over her. She went on to explain: "I guess I had no self-respect. I was afraid to speak up, in case my suspicions were confirmed. So I kept silent. Now I know I made a bad choice."

Today Jamie's mom shudders when she thinks about what happened to her daughter. If she could do it over again, she says she would leave her husband to protect Jamie. Though she can't undo her mistakes, she did ask Jamie for forgiveness.

Jamie and her mother are still working on their relationship, and they haven't found it easy. Many old wounds that needed exposure and cleansing have surfaced. However, now honesty and love provide a firm foundation for their relationship. When winds of adversity shake their lives, they choose to weather the storms together.

For years Jamie imagined her mother disowning her if she brought up the subject of incest. As you can see, her story had a different ending. During therapy she learned some ways to let her imagination work for her, rather than against her. This helped her build courage to face her mother and her offender in person. You, too, can use mental imagery to reduce fear and build confidence.

Use Your Imagination for Your Good!

After several months of counseling, Jamie said, "I think I'm ready to face my offender." This came as no surprise. For months she had been preparing for this confrontation, rehearsing what she needed to say and how she wanted to say it. She felt determined to speak her mind in a firm but loving fashion. With God's help, she knew it was time to take another step forward. We helped her use her imagination to prepare for a positive confrontation and said something like this:

"Jamie, picture yourself as a successful businesswoman. Other people already see you this way. Your head is high, your shoulders are back, and you exude confidence. Everything about you communicates strength and stability. See yourself interacting competently with your associates.

"Now look at your schedule book. When you realize your next appointment is with your offender, your stomach tumbles with fear. However, as you remember Jesus' promise to never leave you, your confidence is immediately boosted. You realize He is with you. As you walk to meet your father, peace fills your heart.

"As you near the room where you'll meet your offender, you pray silently and ask Jesus to give you the courage you need. You feel instantly reassured of His loving support. When you see your offender, you know you will not face him alone.

"Now see yourself speaking to your father using firm, loving words. Be keenly aware of the strength in your body. Communicate everything you have planned and rehearsed. Be open and honest. Do not withdraw. Let kindness season your speech. . . .

"When you complete the confrontation, turn around and walk out the door. Imagine yourself breathing a sigh of relief and sensing a new dimension of healing in your heart. Pause and thank the Lord for His faithfulness and for the promise He made you when He said 'If you come to me when you are weary and burdened, I will give you rest. Let me walk with you and teach you my ways, for I am gentle and humble in heart. With me you will find the rest for your soul' [see Matthew 11:28, 29]."

The following week, when Jamie arrived for counseling, an aura of peace surrounded her. We understood why as she recounted the story of confronting her father: "I used the imagery exercise every day last week while preparing to talk with my father. I knew the Lord was with me. He kept assuring me Dad's response didn't matter. The important thing was that I was taking a step to restore our relationship by confronting him in love. I have done all I can do to restore our relationship. The next move is Dad's."

As Jamie focused upon Christ's ability to give her strength and courage, the task of assimilation became easier. Buoyed by His support, she grew to understand her father's perspectives without compromising her own position. With the help of assimilation exercises, the big picture of her abuse came into focus. Through forgiveness, she experienced emotional healing and a chance for a new relationship with her father.

Confronting Your Offender

It is extremely important to eliminate misconceptions over who is to blame for sexual abuse. Confusion generally clears when a victim confronts her offender and places total responsibility for the offense on him.

One word of caution. You must base your confrontation on careful planning and certain ground rules that will guard you from miscommunicating your message.

When you confront your offender, base your communication upon honesty and integrity. Communicate care. A responsible confrontation is always tempered by love. Let your words show in a respectful way that you want him to know where you stand and what you feel, need, value and want.[5]

As you balance your communication with caring and confronting statements, chances are you'll have a successful interaction. Chart 7 lists some sentences that may guide you as you plan what you need to say and how you want to say it.

Some further suggestions for confronting your offender are outlined below:

Chart 7[6]

Let Your Words Be Caring	Let Your Words Be Confronting
"I care about our relationship."	"I feel deeply about the issue at stake."
"I want to hear your view."	"I want to clearly express mine."
"I trust you to be able to handle my honest feelings."	"I want you to trust me with yours."
"I promise to stay with the discussion until we've reached an understanding."	"I want you to keep working with me until we've reached a new understanding."

Plan the points you want to make beforehand. Write them out and carefully edit each statement. Stick with a few simple points. Make short explanations that clearly describe how you feel. Then share your ideas with a trusted friend and rehearse your presentation.

Use *I statements,* such as "I think," "I feel," and "I believe." For example, you might say, *"I feel* angry that you took advantage of my trust in you," *"I believe* you should have known better," Or, *"I feel* the responsibility for what happened is yours."

Don't use *you statements,* such as, *"You are* a child molester." *"You think* I don't know what you did." Or, *"You blamed* everything on me."

Listen to your offender's perspective. If necessary, repeat what you think you heard him say. Some examples of paraphrasing an offender's comments are shown in Chart 8.

Leave the door open for future interaction. Let your offender know whether or not you want a relationship. Explain the conditions, if there are any.

Focus your feedback on the offense rather than the person. Comment on the offending behavior, rather than criticizing your offender. This affirms his freedom to

Chart 8

Offender Says	Victim Responds
"I had more responsibilities than I could handle at the time."	"You were feeling somewhat overwhelmed with responsibility."
"Nobody understood me."	"It seemed as though no one understood you at the time."
"I took my frustrations out on you."	"You weren't angry at me, but I happened to be handy."

change, instead of stimulating feelings of rejection. "I am angry about the abuse."

Voice your remarks in terms of observations, rather than conclusions. Comment on what you have personally seen, heard, and experienced. Be careful not to draw conclusions that will evoke defensiveness in your offender, such as "You came into my room at night and thought you owned my body."

Describe your offender's actions and behaviors. Be careful not to add value judgments. "I'm aware that you have been silent, and I'm wondering what this means."

Focus your feedback to your offender in the form of ideas and alternatives, rather than advice and answers. "Getting into counseling is one way of helping yourself."

Confrontation Isn't an Absolute Must

Some adult victims struggle with their inability to confront their offender. They may:

Fear negative repercussions and wonder how a confrontation may affect their own relationships with other family members.

Fear others won't believe them.

Not feel strong enough to counter the offender's denial or accusations that may occur in the confrontation.

Not have the option of confronting the offender, due to death or disappearance.

If you cannot contact or confront your offender, do not despair. While confrontation helps many victims, by no means does healing absolutely require it.

Since each victim has her own timetable of healing, the decision to confront rests on a victim's personal assessment of her ability to handle it. Just because one person feels ready to confront her offender doesn't mean *you* have to feel ready now, too. Give yourself enough time to become well prepared and emotionally strong. Take your time. Perhaps, like Melanie, you'll eventually decide to meet your offender face-to-face.

Melanie was in counseling for many months before she made a list of the essential points she wanted to tell her father. After leaving home, she accepted Christ as her personal Lord and Savior and wanted her father to learn about God, too. She worked hard to delicately balance her expression of anger and fear with God's forgiving love. Wanting to be a good testimony for the Lord, in a letter, she approached him this way:

Dad, there are some things I've wanted to share with you for a long time. I love you and must be honest with you. I remember the things you did to me when I was little and we were home alone. You may think I didn't realize what was happening, or you may think I forgot it, but I didn't. Dad, I was terrified of what might happen if I didn't let you touch me in those places. I felt dirty and thought it was all my fault. I was convinced that if I had been a better daughter, you wouldn't have misused me this way.

It's very hard for me to tell you these things. Even now I'm tempted to feel like a bad little girl. But I know that I have to speak the truth in love to you. Please get professional help. I will stand by you and support you as you take the steps to help yourself. This situation was your responsibility then, and it is your responsibility now. Please do something about it.

As he read her letter Melanie's father was moved. Though he knew she had told the truth, he stood to lose everything if he admitted his offenses. He told Melanie he knew the abuse was his fault, but he couldn't seek professional help.

Melanie prays daily that her father will deal with his burden of guilt by seeking psychological and spiritual counseling. As far as she can Melanie has taken active intervention. The ball is now in her father's court. She consistently intercedes for him, contending for his spiritual and emotional healing. Her greatest desire is to see her father restored, as she was, with the help of a loving and forgiving God.

eleven

The Road of Healing

"WILL I EVER GET OVER THIS NIGHTMARE?" LISA asked. "It seems that when I think it's over and I've remembered everything, something else pops up. Just when I make sense out of my past, another rush of confusion sweeps over me. I feel as if I keep getting stuck. There sure aren't any magical cures, are there?"

No, there are no magic potions or quick cures for the emotional pain caused by sexual abuse. But we have good news. Complete and total restoration from childhood sexual abuse can become reality. Both Lisa and you need to take heart. As you walk down the road of recovery, you will find different kinds of healing available to you. Let's look at two ways restoration can occur.

Miracles and Common Healing

One type of restoration is a miracle: God provides an immediate healing, which takes away all the flashbacks and the painful emotions that go with it. If He has done that for you, praise Him for it! He has given you a divine healing, in which He broke through the barriers of nature to bring about a supernatural change.

Most of us want—and sometimes demand—God to perform a divine healing. When it seems as though our prayers bounce off the ceiling and when healing doesn't take place, we may easily become discouraged and immediately assume that God has no interest in helping us. But nothing could be further from the truth.

Remember that God is not locked into our expectations or demands. He says, "As the heavens are higher than the earth, so are my ways higher than your ways and my thoughts than your thoughts" (Isaiah 55:9). In His wisdom, He knows what is best for each individual. Some people, He knows, benefit most from a gradual healing process, and for them He may use common healing to bring wholeness into their lives. Many of the methods discussed in this book are means of common healing. If you believe that God has supplied mankind with knowledge in the medical and psychological sciences, then you may logically assume that He will use these avenues to bring healing to His people.

If you have not received an instantaneous healing, don't lose heart. You have many biblical and psychological helps at your fingertips. Use these tools during your day-to-day walk with

God. As you make an effort to grab and utilize those helps, God will walk with you out of slavery, into freedom.

Yes, it does take time to learn how to use these therapeutic tools, and it requires effort. But in the process, you have the privilege of being involved in a cooperative contract in which you and God work together toward restoration. God wants to comfort and heal the pain of your undeserved abuse. He delights in and will bless every step you take towards wholeness. He will honor your honesty in seeking help.

Catching a Glimpse of Meaning in the Healing Process

For many years you may have struggled with the trauma of your sexual abuse. Perhaps life seems futile, and you see no way out of your dark hole of despair. We want to encourage you to find meaning and purpose in your suffering. Purpose can bring sustenance and strength to your mental and emotional well-being.

One of our clients, Sandy, recently finished a year and a half of group therapy for sexual-abuse victims. At the end of the last session, she recorded some thoughts in her journal. They may help you find meaning in your pain:

Resolution of sexual abuse is not an easy task. I had to examine my feelings, and it was hard, hard work. My real struggle involved clearing the anger, hate, and guilt out of my heart. It was frustrating when I couldn't keep my feelings tidy and controlled.

I saw my first sign of growth when I reopened my heart while talking with a close friend. As I reached out, my pain diminished. My next big hurdle was to make an appointment with a counselor. I never thought I'd have the courage to go through with it. But I did.

When I joined the therapy group for victims, a whole new world opened for me. In the supporting closeness of the group, my feelings were validated. I saw others cry and struggle with anger, guilt, and hatred. I knew I wasn't alone.

As I took the risk of sharing my experiences, good and bad memories floated to the surface. The group accepted and loved me in spite of the ugly parts of my life. With their help, I found the will to laugh, to live, and to love again.

I feel as if I've closed a chapter in my life now. I can lay my past to rest. My abuse is no longer the primary focus of my days. It's just one small piece of the total picture.

Sandy realized that complete healing takes much more than a quick fix. Suffering brought deep changes and growth in her life. This can happen to you as well. In your quest for survivorhood, relief will come when you look for glimpses of meaning in your suffering.

Myths That Stall Progress

Sometimes a victim can be blocked from making progress in healing simply because she entertains misconceptions about recovery. Since this happens frequently, we included two myths that commonly trip up victims.

MYTH 1: *"If I try hard enough, I can overcome my trauma by myself."* Some Christians say, "All I need is God. He and I will go it alone." This viewpoint paralyzes people. In Scripture God never tells us to "go it alone." Instead, the

Bible tells us to be interdependent. This is totally different from secular views, which promote independence and isolation. But our Creator knows our deepest needs and in wisdom provides excellent counsel.

In John 17, just prior to the account of Christ's death and resurrection, Christ prays to God the Father for His disciples and for all other believers. In several of the twenty-six verses in that chapter, He communicates His earnest desire for believers to be united and intimate with one another. "Jesus said this, and looked toward heaven and prayed. . . . I pray for those who will believe in me, that all of them may be one, Father, just as you are in me and I am in you. May they also be in us so that the world may believe that you have sent me. May they be brought to complete unity to let the world know that you sent me and have loved them even as you have loved me" (*see* John 17:1, 20–23).

Not only do Christ's words encourage interdependency, the writer of Hebrews also challenges us to closely relate to others. Hebrews 10:24, 25 says, "And let us consider how we may spur one another on toward love and good deeds. Let us not give up meeting together, as some are in the habit of doing, but let us encourage one another—and all the more as you see the Day approaching."

Paul also tells us to comfort the hurting: ". . . God . . . comforts us in all our troubles, so that we can comfort those in any trouble with the comfort we ourselves have received from God" (2 Corinthians 1:3, 4). If you hurt, give yourself permission to be comforted by your friends. This is part of God's plan for your life.

God always presses his children towards unity, oneness of mind, and interdependency. The nature of this type of a relationship demands openness, transparency, and vulnerability. God has not asked you to be a Lone Ranger Christian. Don't let the myth that to be spiritual, you must go it alone, dupe you.

MYTH 2: *"I must understand everything that happened to me before I can move beyond my victimization and become a survivor."* How untrue! Many victims progress towards survivorhood long before they have all the answers about their past abuse. Others hang on to this myth in order to rationalize and circumvent their responsibility in the healing process; they use this as an excuse for not facing their abuse, loss, and hurt. While we empathize with the discomfort of dealing with sexual abuse, we warn against using this coping strategy, because it keeps victims locked in the past.

God encourages us to trust Him when we don't have all the answers. The Bible says, ". . . Let him who walks in the dark, who has no light, trust in the name of the Lord and rely on his God" (Isaiah 50:10). God promises, "I will counsel you with my eye upon you. . . . Trust in me with all your heart and don't lean on your own understanding. Acknowledge me in all your ways, and I will direct your paths" (*see* Psalms 32:8; Proverbs 3). You may never have all the answers. But you have a God who does. Trust Him to reveal the necessary facts to you, and leave the rest to Him.

You Can Experience Healing

Of all the tragedies of life, the forfeiting of hope and the failure to look forward are the worst. You may feel as if healing is for others, but not for you. Perhaps turmoil has continued for years, and you feel whipped by fatigue and hopelessness.

If you only glean one truth from this book, let it be this: You can become a *survivor* of sexual abuse. Victims can experience life to its fullest, in spite of their past. Complete healing can relieve the tug and tension of old scars and bring full relief from emotional pain.

Why can we promise this? Because God is the author of tomorrows and new beginnings. However, the choice lies with you. You can shrink back and continue to let the trauma of your past violate you, or you can face tomorrow and say, "Okay, Lord. I want to move beyond my victimization. I'm going to lean on You as I go through the healing process. I'm going to trust You one day at a time. Regardless of how I feel each day, I choose to believe that You will bring about a complete restoration in my life as we work together."

Milestones Along the Road to Healing

When you're planning a trip, sometimes it helps to have a road map with marks that will help you keep perspective as you drive. As therapists we like to inform our clients of what they will encounter as they walk down the road of healing. When they know where they are going and can anticipate milestones along the way, it reduces their anxiety. The following markers are usually encountered on a victim's journey of recovery.

Milestone 1—Activation. Activation occurs when a victim first becomes aware of her abuse. This may happen through flashbacks, nightmares, memories, fears, panic, or a general uneasiness in the presence of a particular person. When this first occurs, a victim may be shocked and unable to display emotion. She may feel depressed, tearful, and be unable to concentrate. Appetite and sleep disturbances also are common during activation.

Confusion predominates because the victim can only work with bits and pieces of pain from her past. Since her thinking may not be well organized, she may appear "spaced out." This commonly happens to victims who have just begun to recall memories. They need firm, loving support from a trained helper as they process the events of their abuse and get better acquainted with their feelings.

Milestone 2—Reliving the Pain. During this phase of healing the victim mentally relives her abuse. As she pictures the molestation the way it happened during childhood she feels intense grief and a deep sense of loss. Her body may have stored memories of the abuse within her muscles, especially if the abuse occurred before her verbal skills were developed. Even though the victim may not have been able to express what happened to her at the time, her body and mind still held on to the experiences.

In this stage many victims lose spontaneity, since remembering consumes so much energy and effort. They may experience wide mood swings and a multitude of different feelings in very short periods of time. Preoccupied with their abuse, they need to talk about the past. A strong support system is extremely important, because as memories become more distinct, victims need a lot of "talk time" and tender loving care.

Milestone 3—Seeking Support. During this time victims feel very vulnerable and unprotected. Because they realize their trust in others was grossly violated, they tend to withdraw and run. Often they feel hopeless and have a hard time trusting even those who love them most. Mood swings may become more pronounced. One minute they want to talk, but a moment later they may get angry and close everybody out. A therapy group offering consistent support and education can be especially helpful during this phase of recovery.

Milestone 4—Putting It All Together. As a victim progresses towards healing she begins to see patterns in her behavior, which are connected to her past. What she learns in therapy about the dynamics of abuse, she integrates with her own experience, and she gains a bigger picture of what took place in her life. As she understands the present in light of her past, she makes corrective and healthy choices. Growth becomes apparent, and pain no longer consumes her. After putting pieces of the puzzle together, she is ready to move on with life.

Are You a Survivor or a Victim?

Dimensions of growth become apparent as victims become survivors. In Chart 9 we've outlined a few of the indicators of survivorhood.[1] However, let us caution you. These are not standards against which to measure yourself. Survivorhood evolves as the hurts and pain of the past heal. The Holy Spirit brings these new dimensions of growth in His perfect timing.

As you experience change, praise the Lord for working in you and give yourself a pat on the back. Growth will continue as you choose to stick with God through the healing process. Be patient and have courage. In time you will reap the rewards of your choices.

Crossing the waters of victimization to the shores of survivorhood is no easy task. At least, that's what the victims we have met think. Many, like Erin, despair, thinking they'll never get better. "When will it ever end?" she asked. "I'm working so hard. But the harder I work, the more I find needs to be done. I didn't even want to come to my appointment today, because I feel as if I am going backwards."

Chart 9
Indicators of
Healing

The Survivor	The Victim
Is able to cultivate intimate relationships with the opposite sex without compromising her own identity.	Experiences difficulty in forming relationships with men who don't compromise her.
Draws self-esteem from focusing on her relationship with God and her internal qualities.	Draws her self-esteem from a preoccupation with accomplishments, appearance, and other external qualities.
Experiences healing in her relationships with loved ones who were part of her abuse.	Closes out relationships with loved ones who were part of her abuse.
Is able to assertively, honestly, and directly express feelings and needs to others.	Does not express her feelings and needs directly and honestly.
Cares for herself by establishing a broad support system.	Tends to withdraw from others, rather than asking for support.
Becomes increasingly comfortable in sexual expressions with a loved one.	Is sexually inappropriate, either avoiding sexual expressions altogether or indiscriminately expressing them.
Is comfortable with expressing her personal belief system.	Holds back in expressing beliefs and opinions.
Is able to give and receive healthy expressions of love.	Has difficulty in recognizing healthy expressions of love.

Erin's ambivalence is common. Victims who process their abuse do experience trying times and periodically feel they aren't progressing in recovery. But when they keep working at airing their wounds and tying up the loose ends of their abuse, in time they do recover.

When victims feel like throwing in the towel, helpers can carry hope for them.[2] When victims cannot see their way out of the tunnel and feel too exhausted to move ahead, loved ones can walk beside them and help them look forward. Good and bad days will come. But as victims persevere, one day they'll walk out of their dark tunnel as overcomers, having learned from and moved beyond the pain of their past.

part five

RESPONSIBLE CARING

twelve

Counsel for Loved Ones

WHEN I ENTERED THE OFFICE, A MESSAGE FROM BOB waited for me. After I returned his call, the helplessness many husbands of adult victims feel struck me.

"I just can't seem to get through to her," Bob said in anguish. "I try to help her out of her slumps, but usually end up saying the wrong thing. Sometimes she acts as if *I'm* the one who violated her, instead of her father. I love Rita and want to help, but I don't know how. What can I do?"

I felt Bob's deep frustration and knew how difficult he found it to watch his wife work through the emotional pain of childhood sexual abuse.

Sexual abuse is not an isolated incident: It affects not only the victim, but also her relationships with others. Since isolation and secrecy were so much a part of her past, she has difficulty communicating. This leaves husbands and other loved ones feeling shoved aside and confused in their endeavors to help.[1]

We'd like to give helpers some tips on how they can aid those who have been or are being sexually abused. First let's take a look at the potential indicators of sexual abuse.

How to Know When Sexual Abuse Is Happening to Children

We frequently hear the questions, "How can I tell if someone is an abuse victim? Are there specific signs to look for?" The answer is yes! Signs of sexual abuse fall into three general categories: behavior signs, family signs, and physical signs.[2]

Behavior signs are probably the easiest to spot. Often victims express the feelings they can't verbalize through subtle actions. At times children give clues through behavior, rather than words. The following list of indicators can help sensitize you to the possibilities of a child's being sexually abused.

Behavioral Indicators of Sexual Abuse
in Infants and Preschoolers[3]

1. Being uncomfortable around previously trusted persons

2. Sexualized behavior (excessive masturbation, sexually inserting objects, explicit sex play with other children, etc.)

3. Fear of restrooms, showers, or baths (common locations of abuse)

4. Fear of being alone with men or boys

5. Nightmares on a regular basis or about the same person

6. Abrupt personality changes

7. Uncharacteristic hyperactivity

8. Moodiness, excessive crying

9. Aggressive or violent behavior toward other children

10. Difficulty in sleeping or relaxing

11. Clinging behavior that may take the form of separation anxiety

12. Passive or withdrawn behavior

The indicators listed above pertain to *changes* in a child's behavior. Any one or more of these behaviors may characterize a child who is not being abused. However, when dramatic changes in a child's behavior occur in alignment with these indicators, loved ones should feel concern.

Children are sexual beings, and you may expect sexual curiosity from an early age. However when a child becomes obsessively preoccupied with the activities we've listed, the time has come for further investigation.

My friend Joan felt concerned about Timmy, her three-year-old. She caught Timmy playing "doctor" with his three-year-old cousin Jenny. Joan wasn't sure whether she should be concerned and turned to me for advice. I assured her that sexual curiosity between preschool children was perfectly natural. She didn't make a big deal out of Timmy's "doctoring." Once he had satisfied his curiosity, no further incidents occurred.

However, Terri's little boy, Randy, was a victim of child molestation. Randy was four when Stan, his fifteen-year-old cousin, baby-sat each week. During the first couple of months Randy loved Stan coming to the house. But after three months Randy hid behind his mom or ran to his room when Stan came to baby-sit. When Terri and Randy visited Stan's family, Randy clung to Terri and refused to play with the other children. Perplexed by Randy's behavior, Terri finally asked him why he was scared of Stan. Randy said, "Stan hurt me down there," pointing to his penis. When Terri asked him to be more specific, Randy said, "Stan rubbed my tinkler so hard it hurt." Terri told her sister, and they confronted Stan together. Fortunately, both Stan and Randy received help before it was too late.

Behavioral Indicators of Sexual Abuse In Latency-Age Children[4]

1. Being uncomfortable around someone previously trusted

2. Specific knowledge of sexual facts and terminology beyond developmental age

3. Sexualized behavior (excessive masturbation, sexual acting out with other children on a regular basis, seductive toward peers and adults, etc.)

4. Wearing multiple layers of clothing, especially to bed

5. Parentified behavior (pseudo-mature, acts like a small parent)

6. Fear of being alone with men or boys

7. Fear of rest rooms, showers or baths

8. Constant, unexplained anxiety, tension or fear

9. Frequent tardiness or absence from school, especially if male caretaker writes excuses

10. Attempts to make herself ugly or undesirable (such as poor personal hygiene)

11. Eating disorders (obesity, bulimia, anorexia)

12. Self-conscious behavior, especially regarding body

13. Reluctance to go home after school

14. Abrupt personality changes

15. Child acquires toys or money with no explanation

16. Wetting of bed or clothing after being "broken" of that problem

17. Nightmares on a regular basis or about the same person

18. Change in sleeping habits (tries to stay up late or seems constantly tired)

19. Moodiness, inappropriate crying

20. Unusual need for assurance of love

21. Regressive behavior (fantasies and/or infantile behavior)

22. Uncharacteristic aggressive or violent behavior

23. Tendency to seek out or totally avoid adults

24. Inability to relate to peers

25. Running away, especially in a child normally not a behavioral problem

Nanci had been an exceptional student prior to sixth grade. She was vivacious, pretty, and popular. But during the first few months of sixth grade the school guidance counselor noticed changes in her behavior and appearance. She had had outstanding attendance records in previous years, but now rarely made it to class. When she did attend, she seemed unable to concentrate on her studies.

Nanci's appearance went from neat to messy, and her counselor wondered what was wrong. She approached Nanci after school one day and asked if something was bothering her. Nanci didn't answer the question directly, but seemed to be glad for a chance to talk. Eventually the counselor asked Nanci if things were all right at home. Nanci's countenance dropped, and after some prodding, she confessed she was being abused by her dad.

Many of the indicators of sexual abuse in latency-age children are similar to those for adolescents. The distinguishing key, a change in Nanci's behavior, tipped off her counselor to possible problems at home. Children frequently communicate through their actions, especially when they have been warned not to talk about the abuse. Keep this in mind as we look at indicators in adolescents.

Behavioral Indicators of Sexual Abuse in Adolescents[5]

1. Sexualized behavior (promiscuity, prostitution, sexual abuse of younger children, etc.)

2. Running away, especially in a child normally not a behavioral problem

3. Drug and alcohol abuse

4. Suicidal gestures or attempts

5. Self-mutilation

6. Extreme hostility toward a parent or caretaker

7. Parentified behavior (pseudo-mature, acts like a small parent)

8. Self-conscious behavior, especially regarding body

9. Wearing multiple layers of clothing, especially to bed

10. Eating disorders (usually obesity)

11. Nightmares and other sleeping problems

12. Constant fear or anxiety

13. Delinquent behavior

14. School problems (academic or behavioral)

15. Defiance or compliance to an extreme

16. Friends tend to be older

I met Tina in the psychiatric ward of a nearby hospital. Her arms were filled with superficial scars, which the chief psychiatrist called ''hesitation marks.'' When Tina felt ambivalent about killing herself, cutting her arms seemed to make her feel better. She felt she needed to be punished for being sexually abused. Cutting her arms seemed to diminish the bad feelings she had about herself.

At the age of seventeen Tina had attempted suicide several times. After she had repeatedly run away from home, Children's Protective Services placed her with a foster family. Her counselor soon learned that during her early teenage years Tina had been continually abused by her mother's boyfriends. Running away and suicide attempts were simply efforts to escape a living hell. Fortunately her counselor listened and believed Tina's story and helped her make a clean break from home.

Professionals and loved ones *must* calmly listen to children who show signs of sexual abuse. Most of all these children need the safety and security that an atmosphere of quiet encouragement can foster. When children sense that parents or helpers will react negatively to the truth, they will keep their "secrets" to themselves.

If you suspect a member of your family or a friend is being molested, seek help. Professional counselors who specialize in child abuse and staff members at Children's Protective Services Agencies are trained to interview children without causing unnecessary upset. If you notice behavior changes like the ones we've mentioned, don't close your eyes and pretend nothing is wrong. Undoubtedly something is wrong, and you owe it to the suspected victim to find out. Be alert to the indicators of molestation in children, as well as in adults.

Adult Behavioral Indicators of Sexual Abuse

Many adult women molested as children do not connect their early abuse with later problems in life. Because they have such a sophisticated denial system, they find it hard to sort out why they struggle with emotional problems and relationship hassles. However, when asked directly about sexual abuse, usually victims can recite their history of molestation.[6] Below we have listed behavioral indicators that suggest sexual abuse may have occurred.

Behavioral Indicators of Sexual Abuse in Adults[7]

1. Sexual difficulties (usually regarding intimacy issues)

2. Distrust of the opposite sex

3. Inappropriate choice of partners (chooses a dependent partner she can mother or one who abuses her or her children physically or sexually)

4. Progressive breakdown of communication and eventual emotional detachment from children

5. Multiple marriages

6. Extreme dependence upon or anger toward a parent

7. Sexual promiscuity (or alternating between periods of preoccupation with or revulsion by sexual activity)

8. Drug or alcohol abuse

9. Extremely low self-esteem

10. Nightmares or flashbacks

11. Continual victimization (seemingly unable to assert or protect self)

12. May see self-worth only in sexuality

13. Eating disorders

14. Self-punishing behaviors

15. Homosexual orientation

16. Body shame (extreme self-consciousness)

By the time abuse victims have reached adulthood, behaviors that have served to cover their pain may have become a pronounced part of their personalities. Tread lightly if you suspect an adult loved one was a childhood victim. Create an atmosphere that allows her to come to you with the secret. (We'll discuss more do's and don'ts later on.)

Familial Indicators of Child Sexual Abuse

Sometimes friends and loved ones can detect family indicators that suggest sexual abuse. However, this is usually a difficult task, because most families involved in sexual abuse are secretive and put up a good front for others. Therefore the victim still provides the best source of information for suspected abuse.[8] Below we have listed family indicators that suggest the existence of sexual abuse:

Family Indicators of Sexual Abuse[9]

1. Role reversal between mother and daughter

2. Extreme overprotectiveness or jealousy toward a child by a parent (parent sharply restricts a child's contact with peers and adults outside the home)

3. Inappropriate sleeping arrangements (child sleeps with a parent on a regular basis or with both parents, where she is exposed to sexual activity)

4. Prolonged absence of one parent from the home (through death, divorce, etc.) so the child may be forced to fill the absent partner's role

5. Mother who is often ill or disabled

6. Extreme lack of communication between caretakers

7. Inordinate participation of father in family (father may interact very little with family members or may insist on being in charge of all family activities)

8. Extreme paternal dominance of spouse (for instance, mother is not allowed to drive or to talk to school personnel, etc.)

9. Work or activity schedules that result in a caretaker (especially male) spending large amounts of time alone with a child or children

10. Extreme favoritism shown to a child (father may spend a lot of time giving attention to one daughter)

11. Severe overreaction by a parent to any sex education offered a child

12. Caretaker who has been sexually abused as a child

13. Geographic isolation of family

14. Overcrowding in a home so that children are forced to sleep with parents and/or other family members

15. Family has no social or personal support system

16. Alcohol or drug abuse within a family

When it comes to evaluating potential abuse situations, take caution: jumping to an extreme and seeing a case under every rock could cause much harm. Uneducated accusations not based on facts can wreak havoc in relationships. At the same time, do not let clear facts go unnoticed, as society in general and the Christian church in particular have often allowed to happen.

The average Christian finds it difficult to accept the fact that sexual abuse occurs in Christian families. Sometimes we all need a challenge to become involved. How easy to say, "It's none of my business!" or, "Why open a can of worms?" As responsible care givers, we must resist the temptation to ignore signs of child abuse. Assuming that Christian families have an immunity to this aspect of our fallen world is simply spiritual naiveté.[10]

Physical Indicators of Abuse

Behavioral indicators communicate powerful messages. When the signs correctly indicate abuse, physical evidence will also support the truth.

Loved ones need to be aware of the symptoms listed below which can provide conclusive or corroborative evidence that a child has been sexually victimized.

Physical Indicators of Sexual Abuse[11]

1. Pain or itching in the genital area

2. Difficulty in walking or sitting

3. Vaginal discharge

4. Bruises or bleeding of external genitalia, vaginal or anal regions

5. Venereal disease, especially in young children

6. Swollen or red cervix, vulva, or perineum

7. Pregnancy, when a child refuses to reveal any information about the father or there is a complete denial of pregnancy by the child or her parents

8. Torn, stained or bloody underclothing

9. Unusual and offensive odors

We have included these categorizations of behavioral, familial, and physical indicators to help loved ones end the sex-abuse nightmare. Parents, helpers and counselors can stop molestation by looking for signals and diligently investigating when suspicion is aroused. Adult awareness and sensitivity can prevent single incidents of abuse from becoming a long-term pattern. We owe children this.

How to Prevent Abuse

By speaking openly about the subject with children who are potential victims, adults can best prevent child abuse. Children learn through direct teaching and positive role modeling. To help you, we've provided four important concepts adults can share with youngsters:[12]

1. Be aware of how you feel about other people. When someone treats you differently from the way you think you should be treated, you'll probably sense an "uh-oh" feeling inside.

2. Sometimes people try to trick us into sharing our bodies. They may offer us something we want, like a toy or friendship, if we share our private parts with them.

3. When you don't feel good about how someone treats you, remember three very important words: *no, go* and *tell*. It's okay to say no to someone, if he wants you to share your body. It's also important to go and tell someone else if another person asks you for these bad favors.

4. Speak up for yourself. If you have a problem, others will help you. All you have to do is tell them. Unless you tell them, they may not know you are hurting.

Teach children to be sensitive to the "uh-oh" feeling that comes when others try to touch their private body parts. Alert them to certain "tricks" people use, and convince them that their bodies are private property and nobody has a right to trespass. If children learn that sexual abuse is always the offender's fault, chances are they will feel less fearful about disclosing the truth. Adults can also prevent sexual abuse by:

Telling children not to accept anything from strangers.

Telling children not to open the door to anyone, when their parents are not at home.

Telling children to talk with them if family members or friends make them feel uncomfortable.

Closely watching older family members who spend time exclusively with younger children.

Knowing their children's bodies. Being alert to any physical changes.

Observing their children's behavior and moods. Being curious about mood swings and quick changes in personality.

Not only children need to learn to monitor "uh-oh" feelings. Adult victims also can benefit from sensitizing themselves to these feelings when they're involved in relationships.

Some adult victims have endured multiple incidents of sexual abuse, but they can prevent reabuse if they tune into "uh-oh" feelings when they sense misuse may happen again. If they suspect a violation is about to happen, they must speak up for themselves. Just because a victim was abused during childhood does not mean she has to accept abuse in adulthood. Everyone has the right to say no when someone asks for inappropriate sexual favors. We owe this to ourselves.

What to Do When a Child Reports Sexual Abuse

As a policeman and experienced sexual abuse consultant, Gary Strudler offers some excellent advise to those who receive reports of child abuse:[13]

1. Temper your reactions. Remember children will evaluate your responses. Do your best not to overreact or display shock or horror.

2. Above all, believe the child who is reporting to you. Children rarely lie about sexual abuse.

3. Commend the child for telling you and convey your support.

4. Reassure the child that he or she is not to blame or at fault. It is of paramount importance to alleviate self-blame.

5. Let the child know what you are going to do.

6. Report to the proper authorities.

7. Do not promise not to tell.

We also encourage family counseling in order to diminish potential lifelong adjustment problems—and the sooner the better. Early intervention and therapy can help ensure a better prognosis for complete recovery.

How to Support the Adult Victim of Child Sexual Abuse

Most people don't feel comfortable with the subject of sexual abuse. Hearing adult victims share about past abuse can make us feel put on the spot—we don't know what to say, our minds go blank, and in an effort to say something, a sort of mumbo jumbo bursts out of our mouths. When our ears actually hear what we've said, we want to crawl under a chair and hide. In embarrassment we think *That wasn't what I meant to say!*

Not everyone is familiar with the dynamics of sexual abuse. Some Christians think sexual abuse never happens to Christians. Still others interpret the effects of abuse, like depression and anger, as sin or a lack of faith. Because of these misunderstandings, adult victims are often at the receiving end of abrasive, flippant remarks. At other times responders simply reply indifferently or evasively. As a result of these insensitive reactions, adult victims often choose to deny their feelings and suffer in silence.

In most cases, adult victims have an overwhelming need to just be heard and believed. Listening without offering advice or value judgments is a precious gift that anyone can give. Janet told me about her friend Rachel. After twenty years of carrying her "secret," Janet confided in Rachel. "Rachel was wonderful. Her calmness and quiet interest stilled my anxiety. She didn't offer me pat answers or preach a sermon. She just sat quietly and held my hand as I opened part of my life to her. Together we laughed and cried and her eyes told me she cared. She never offered me advice, but she did say, 'I wish I could help you feel better. Can you tell me how I can help?'

"I only really needed to know that Rachel believed me. For so many years I had thought my story wasn't worth anybody's time."

During her recovery, Rachel was extremely supportive to Janet. She did not try to presume Janet's needs. Instead she asked Janet specific questions about how to help.

Many well-meaning friends often try to take charge and rescue victims from their pain. While her heart's intent was right, June's friend Jan suffered from the "rescuer syndrome." When June told Jan about her abuse, Jan gave up all her personal time to be with June. She attempted to comfort her, but ended up stepping on toes and interfering with June's marriage. She also tried to force June to think positive when she was hurting.

June just really needed someone to listen. Reflecting on it, she said, "I think Jan felt afraid of my pain. I know she thought she was doing me a favor by trying to keep my mind off the past, but I needed to face some things before I could put the abuse behind me."

Adult victims need encouragement to help themselves. They need to be allowed to grieve over their losses. They need the freedom to disclose feelings. Professional counselors can help them understand their emotions; however, caring friends and family can provide a sounding board when these feelings surface.

Many people want to know the best ways to help their abused loved one. They also ask, "Is there anything I shouldn't do?" Our experience shows some definite do's and don'ts exist in providing healthy support to victims. We've provided a list of these in Chart 10.

Family members and friends of victims don't have an easy task. It is hard to stand by and watch people you love hurt. But in some ways you can help diminish their pain.

Victims feel supported not so much by what others say, but

Chart 10
Supporting the Adult Victim
of Sexual Abuse

Do	Don't
Do talk with them privately rather than in front of others.	Don't display horror, shock, or disapproval.
Do keep what a victim shares confidential.	Don't pry into unrelated family matters.
Do be a good listener with your eyes and ears.	Don't place blame or judgment on the victim.
Do provide reassurance in your words and body language. A hug says a lot!	Don't give advice as to how victims should solve their problems.
Do advise victims of community resources where they can receive help.	Don't ask *why* questions.
Do help victims follow through with counseling. Attend the first session if they desire.	Don't make sexual abuse into a spiritual problem.
Do remind victims that God loves them and wants to heal and restore them.	Don't force victims to talk about their recovery process. Let them initiate.
Do tell victims repeatedly of your love for them, especially when they feel unlovable.	Don't force victims to think positive. A period of grieving is necessary for recovery to occur.
Do expect many emotional ups and downs during recovery.	Don't impose your timetable for healing on victims. God is working in them at His pace.

more by knowing they have been heard and lovingly accepted. The book of James tells us we should always be quick to listen and slow to speak (James 1:19). Proverbs tells us, "A word aptly spoken is like apples of gold in settings of silver" (25:11). As loved ones rely on God to help them know when to speak and what to say, He will use them to bring healing to victims. In the process both victims and helpers will grow, and God will be glorified.

thirteen

What About the Christian Offender?

H E SAYS HE'S A CHRISTIAN. BUT A CHRISTIAN WOULD never molest his own daughter, would he? How can someone who claims to be a believer sexually abuse a child? There are no easy answers for these difficult questions. The words *Christian* and *offender* seem polar opposites. However, our experience and research show that sexual abuse does occur within Christian circles.[1]

My Spiritual Life Is A Separate Issue!

As we mentioned in chapter 4, offenders distort reality with fragmented thinking. They may attend church on Sunday, molest on Monday and Tuesday, and be back in church on Wednesday. By compartmentalizing and neatly separating spirituality from their homelife, they manage to maintain a fictional life of upstanding fatherhood.

Some incest victims say their fathers were deacons in church and highly respected members of the community. However, children like Janet saw a different side of Dad: "While I was growing up, my dad insisted we all attend church each Sunday. He beamed with pride, showing off his family. It all seemed extremely hypocritical to me. Dad acted holy on Sunday, but before the week was over took advantage of me and my sister. Everyone in our town thought he was a perfect Christian father.

"I never talked to people about what Dad was really like. They wouldn't have believed me anyway. Why should they? Dad looked as if he had it all together. I was just a scrawny little kid who jumped if anyone said, 'Boo!'

"My insides churned when people bragged about him. It was even worse when Mom believed them. Only my sister and I knew the truth. I wish I had been courageous enough to expose him. Perhaps my life wouldn't be as topsy-turvy today, if I had gone to the authorities."

Janet's story illustrates how appearances can deceive. Offenders usually don't notice inconsistencies in their life-styles. Tim's story further illustrates how an offender's fragmented thinking splits his spiritual life and his behavior into two mutually exclusive domains. As he talked with me one evening he asked, "Are you a Spirit-filled Christian?"

As I answered him, I puzzled over what lay behind his question. When he found that I had a personal relationship with the Lord Jesus Christ, he tried to convince me he was unique and special because he, too, was a believer: "Because they aren't Christians, the people from Children's Protective Services don't understand me. I know you'll understand, since Jesus is your Lord. I've asked God to heal me and firmly believe He has answered my prayer. But that stupid agency treats me like every other molester in town. They're making me live away from home and are even talking about a jail sentence. They don't understand that God has already freed me from this sin. There's nothing to worry about now. I've been healed."

Offenders such as Tim minimize the seriousness of their sexual behavior in light of their profession of faith. While denying the reality of his offensive behavior, Tim tried to convince me of his "uniqueness." He had no empathy for the pain and humiliation he had inflicted upon his daughters. Skirting the consequences was his sole concern.

Somehow Tim felt that his membership in God's family exempted him from the natural consequences of his actions. He said he was not like every other molester in town and indignantly objected to being treated as a common child abuser. However, God requires Tim to take his behavior very seriously and to highly regard the effects of his ungodly actions. The Lord never looks lightly at sin, especially when innocent victims can become further exploited if the sin isn't handled.

What Does Research Show Us?

What possible correlation exists between the offender and religion? Surprisingly, research has shown that:

1. Many sex offenders raised in homes with fundamentalist religious teachings believe that any kind of sexual activity is dirty.[2]

2. Some offenders are devoutly religious, moralistic, and highly intent on marrying a virgin.[3]

3. Incest offenders are the most religious group found among sexual abusers.[4]

4. A large proportion of molesters indicate high degrees of religiosity, but come from backgrounds where sexual morality was publicly supported but privately breached.

Jim came from the last type of family and recalls childhood memories: "My father was the mayor of our small town. Everyone respected and admired him. Each Sunday morning he sat in the second row of the First Baptist Church. But I knew the real truth about Dad. I watched him flirt with my aunt and then with my own sisters, when they reached their teens. He had a tremendous amount of power over women. No one knew about his little affairs on the side. Dad taught me that it was okay to be less than lily white, as long as you kept up appearances."

What does research actually tell us? While studies provide evidence of a high degree of religious interest among sex offenders, it remains unclear whether these offenders have actually made a commitment to Christ. Only God knows the hearts of men. It is also unclear, from the research, whether the offenders' conversions took place before or after the discovery of sexual abuse. For these reasons, helpers must evaluate how an offender regards his religious commitment and find out what Christianity actually means to him. No assumptions can be made.

Taking Stock of Offender Motivation

Since his thinking errors cause deception, helpers can have a hard time evaluating an offender's beliefs in God. But one fact stands firm: Regardless of whether or not an offender is Christian, he is definitely more externally controlled than internally motivated.[5] In other words he feeds on external cues, constraints, and direction for life, rather than on internal morals and rules.

Helpers must become aware that an offender cannot move from external motivation to internal motivation overnight. This is the main reason offenders need to be promptly removed from the home. External constraints have to be consistently exercised for long periods of time before they become internalized. Internal consistency between belief and behavior develops slowly. Any attempts to shortcut this process leads to disastrous results for victims and their families.

When untrained helpers excuse wrong behavior and shield offenders from consequences because of a conversion experience, abusers do not change. Instead the "help" reinforces their sinful behavior. They become more confident in their abilities to dupe authorities and end up more deeply in bondage.

God wants those in helping positions to be responsible care givers, which involves speaking the truth in love to offenders and victims. As well as spiritual counsel, sex abusers need professional psychological help. A holistic therapeutic approach that addresses their mental, emotional, and spiritual needs benefits them most.

For effective intervention to occur, sexual conflicts that trap offenders must be examined. Reality distortions and twisted thinking patterns must also be challenged and reoriented before transformation can take place. As offenders learn to function in an environment with consistent external constraints, over time they can develop internal constraints.

Offenders must learn that God loves them and wants to actively release His healing power in their lives. However, He can only do this as they acknowledge their wrong and turn to Him for help.

They must also understand that God is not only loving, merciful and kind; He is also a God of truth and justice. Out of this perfect balance in His character He disciplines His beloved children. Scripture says, "Our fathers disciplined us for a little while as they thought best; but God disciplines us for our good, that we may share in his holiness. No discipline seems pleasant at the time, but painful. Later on, however, it produces a harvest of righteousness and peace for those who have been trained by it" (Hebrews 12:10, 11).

One of the ways God brings healing into our lives is through disciplinary actions. The writer of Hebrews says: ". . . My son, do not make light of the Lord's discipline, and do not lose heart when he rebukes you, because the Lord disciplines those he loves, and he punishes everyone he accepts as a son" (Hebrews 12:5, 6). As a responsible, loving Father, God disciplines His children in order to heal their twisted minds and cultivate the fruits of the Spirit in their character. He may discipline us by allowing us to suffer the natural consequences of our sinful choices.

Opening the Door for Recovery

Offenders perpetuate their problems when they deny, hide, and refuse to deal with their inappropriate sexual behavior. Minimizing, blaming, rationalizing, and justifying do not fool an all-knowing God! Molesters must learn to take responsibility for their actions and be allowed to bear the natural consequences of their behavior. This is a key in the recovery process for any offender, Christian or non-Christian. The following steps can help them learn these lessons and open the door for recovery:

1. *All* sexual activity between the offender and victim must cease.

2. The Children's Protective Services must be notified. With legal authority they will see the offender gets the help he needs. Since offenders skillfully manipulate and convince family members that a problem doesn't exist, trained professionals must be contacted. Ninety-nine percent of the time a problem does exist, when the signs we discussed in chapter 12 are evident.

3. For the victim's protection, she and her offender must be separated. Usually this means the offender needs to leave the home, rather than the underage victim. However, most Children's Protective Services will remove the child immediately upon notification of abuse and return her to the home once the offender has departed.

4. Don't believe the offender when he says, "If you won't report it, I swear it will never happen again." It *will* happen again and again, unless he gets help.

5. Place the blame where it belongs, on the adult offender. Reassure the victim that it isn't her fault.

6. Encourage the entire family to get help. Sexual abuse occurs in dysfunctional families, and everyone involved needs to learn new ways of relating within the home. Search for a competent, trained counselor who specializes in sexual-abuse problems.

Those who minister to offenders need to be caring and confrontational. Irresponsible care giving minimizes offender behavior and buffers penalties. If you really want to help an offender, make no apologies for being direct. Your tough love is in his best interest.

As an offender accepts the truth about himself and makes attitude and behavior changes, chances are he will be restored. However, he will need firm, loving support and regular account-ability as he takes these steps. He must acknowledge his sin and ask forgiveness from his victim, but the buck doesn't stop there. In addition he must receive assistance toward the ultimate goal: a life-style absent of more offenses.

The Church Can Promote Healing!

Offenders need spiritual support, along with professional therapy. Sound biblical teaching and loving fellowship are two primary tools God uses to transform lives. As He takes the offender through a gradual healing process, the church must cooperate with God's purposes and not judge, stigmatize, or reject him. While he recovers, an offender desperately needs support from Christian friends and acceptance in a local body.

In the book of 1 Corinthians Paul writes to the believers in Corinth about incest in the church. He says:

> *It is actually reported that there is sexual immorality among you, and of a kind that does not occur even among pagans: A man has his father's wife. And you are proud! Shouldn't you rather have been filled with grief and have put out of your fellowship the man who did this? Even though I am not physically present, I am with you in spirit. And I have already passed judgment on the one who did this, just as if I were present. When you are assembled in the name of our Lord Jesus and I am with you in spirit, and the power of our Lord Jesus is present, hand this man over to Satan, so that the sinful nature may be destroyed and his spirit saved on the day of the Lord. . . .*

But now I am writing you that you must not associate with anyone who calls himself a brother but is sexually immoral or greedy, an idolator or a slanderer, a drunkard or a swindler. With such a man do not even eat. What business is it of mine to judge those outside the church? Are you not to judge those inside? God will judge those outside. "Expel the wicked man from among you."

1 Corinthians 5:1–5, 11–13

Paul is disgusted with the sexual immorality happening within the church and distressed over the people's attitude towards this issue. He tells the fellowship to disassociate the man who committed the wrong from their gatherings. However, later, in Paul's second letter to the Corinthian church, he commands the believers to forgive and restore that same offender:

The punishment inflicted on him by the majority is sufficient for him [the sexual offender]. Now instead, you ought to forgive and comfort him, so that he will not be overwhelmed by excessive sorrow. I urge you, therefore, to reaffirm your love for him.

2 Corinthians 2:6–8

Paul's directive illustrates the proper balance we need within the Christian church today. Unfortunately, many fellowships exhibit one extreme or the other, either tolerating sexual abuse and taking no corrective action or rejecting offenders with such severity that healing is hindered.

The church today needs to practice loving discipline that results in restoration. As an offender demonstrates repentance, takes responsibility for his abuse, sticks with treatment, and humbly bears the natural consequences of his sin, others must welcome him back into the fellowship. This welcoming process needs to go beyond a simple, "Hi! It's nice to see you," from the pastor on Sunday morning. The offender needs to be incorporated into an existing care group, growth group, or Bible study where he can receive the support and fellowship of other Christians.

Reaffirming, as Paul describes it, involves initiating contact with the offender and inviting him to functions where he can receive acceptance and build friendships. It means providing service opportunities that help him take his mind off himself. Cutting the church lawn, running errands, assisting with building maintenance, or visiting those in nursing homes can be tools used to break his sexual obsession.

As a church brings an offender back into fellowship restoration will happen slowly. Pastors must guard against overwhelming him with too many responsibilities and take caution in placing him in positions where he may have regular contact with children. During the healing process, he remains vulnerable. Specific constraints will provide security and set him up for success rather than failure.

Caring helpers must also directly confront recovering offenders when they make unwise choices. Randy had been in therapy for six weeks when he tried persuading his wife to let him return home. Although he had made progress, in our professional opinion we felt it was too soon for him to go home. We did not feel convinced Randy had internalized a new set of godly behaviors in just six weeks. As we voiced our concerns Randy tried to calm our fears, assuring us he had learned his lesson. But our gut-level instincts told us something different. We recommended he not return home until he had demonstrated his new way of life for twelve months. We expressed our caring concern for him and our desire to see him succeed and not fail.

At the end of the session, Randy reluctantly agreed not to badger his wife any longer. Even though our decision disappointed him, he persevered and consistently worked on changing his attitudes and actions. He participated in group therapy with other offenders and attended family counseling each week. All the legal guidelines laid down as conditions of probation were strictly followed. After twelve months, Randy made periodic visits home; after a sixteen-month separation, finally, he moved back in with his family.

The church played an extremely important part in Randy's recovery process. Initially, his pastor forbade him to attend any fellowship gatherings. However, after Randy's repentance was clearly evident and his pastor saw his progress in therapy, with open arms he welcomed him back to the church. The pastor met regularly with Randy, lending spiritual guidance and support. He also educated his staff and congregation about the importance of helping the weak, using passages such as:

Accept him whose faith is weak. . . .

Romans 14:1

Brothers, if someone is caught in a sin, you who are spiritual should restore him gently. But watch yourself, or you also may be tempted.

Galatians 6:1

My brothers, if one of you should wander from the truth and someone should bring him back, remember this: Whoever turns a sinner away from the error of his way will save him from death and cover over a multitude of sins.

James 5:19, 20

The church is one of God's primary instruments for bringing healing to offenders. They need believers to support them and to lovingly confront them. Early in the recovery process, offenders need help spotting potential pitfalls. Caring friends can help them with foresight. Total restoration is possible when offenders take personal responsibility for their actions and when the church provides a healing atmosphere. Both ingredients are necessary for genuine recovery to occur.

Happy Endings Are Possible!

Sexual abuse is not an unforgivable sin. Jesus died as much for the sins of the offender as for the sins of all mankind. However, forgiveness and healing are gifts. Ultimately the ball drops in the offender's court. Each individual must choose to follow God, in order to benefit from His supernatural restoring power.

Unfortunately, Gerald ignored the hope and encouragement his counselor, pastor, and church family offered. Today he remains embittered and alone, away from his family. While refusing to take responsibility for the abuse, Gerald withered away into despair and lost everything of value to him.

Fred chose a route towards a happy ending. When his wife, June, discovered him in bed with their seven-year-old daughter, she gave him an ultimatum: "Either you get counseling this week, or our marriage is over!"

Eighteen months after entering therapy, Fred said: "The best thing June ever did was to stand her ground. She is small in size, but when she laid down the law about counseling, she was invincible! At first I thought she was trying to punish me, so I pouted. It didn't work."

When June called Derek, their pastor, Fred responded with fury. He felt their family problems were nobody else's business. Pastor Derek, a no-nonsense type of guy, refused to let Fred off the hook. He came with him for his first counseling appointment and supported Fred through the entire recovery process. Reluctantly Fred signed a release-of-information form so that we could talk with Derek about Fred's sessions.

When we reported Fred to the Children's Protective Services, he hated us. But now that sixteen months have passed, he sees things in a different way. One afternoon he said, "I guess it was good for me to serve some time in jail. I've learned not to take my freedom for granted. I've also learned to respect others and to realize that my daughter deserves having a father who doesn't misuse her. That's why I'm not living at home yet. I want to make sure that I've really got this problem under control. I also want my daughter to feel confident about my changes."

Even though Fred doesn't live with his family, he knows he has their support. They attend church and Bible study together each week. When he shares with his Christian friends and admits his need for their love and support, they are there for him. Because people care, Fred knows more today about God's abundant love and life-changing power than he did before his wife discovered the abuse. He has hope for his future, as you can tell from his comment: "Someday, I believe God will completely restore our family. But for now, I'm just taking life one day at a time and focusing on being obedient to Him." Happy endings are possible.

Pamela Vredevelt and Kathryn Rodriguez frequently speak at retreats and conferences. You may contact them at:

Christian Counseling Services
2010 SE 182nd St.
Portland, OR 97232
(503) 566–8832

APPENDIX I
APPENDIX II
SOURCE NOTES

Appendix I

Relaxation Exercises

Quieting Response Exercise

Practice while sitting, standing, driving a car, and so on.

Whenever you encounter a stressful situation and wish to relax, check your breathing. If it is shallow and coming from your upper chest, this indicates that you could be holding tension. Next, take a slow, easy deep breath (from your abdomen), a count of four in, and easy count of four out. Now take another easy breath, a count of four in, and as you exhale to an easy count of four, let your body go totally limp, dropping your jaw, letting it go limp, letting your lips go limp, imagining feelings of warmth and heaviness flowing from your neck down to your toes, reaching your toes at about the same time you have finally let the breath out. Then carry on your normal activity.

Relaxation Exercise

Take a nice deep breath, close your eyes, and begin to relax. Just think about relaxing every muscle in your body, from the top of your head to the tips of your toes. Just begin to relax. And begin to notice how very comfortable your body is beginning to feel. You are supported, so you can just let go and relax. Inhale and exhale. Notice your breathing; notice the rhythm of your breathing and relax your breathing for a moment. Be aware of normal sounds around you. These sounds are unimportant, discard them; whatever you hear from now on will only help to relax you. And as you exhale, release any tension, any stress from any part of your body, mind, and thought; just let that stress go. Just feel any stressful thoughts rushing through your mind, feel them begin to wind down, wind down, wind down, and relax. And begin with letting all the muscles in your face relax, especially your jaw; let your teeth part just a little bit and relax this area. This is a place where tension and stress gather so be sure to relax your jaw and feel that relaxation go into your temples, and relax the muscles in your temples and as you think about relaxing these muscles they will relax. Feel them relax, and as you relax you'll be able to just drift and float into a deeper and deeper level of total relaxation. You will continue to relax, and now let all of the muscles in your forehead relax. Feel those muscles smooth, smooth and relaxed, and rest your eyes. Just imagine your eyelids feeling so comfortable, so heavy, so heavy, so relaxed, and now let all the muscles in the back of your neck and shoulders relax; feel a heavy, heavy weight being lifted off your shoulders, and you feel relieved, lighter and more relaxed. And all of the muscles in the back of your neck and shoulders relax, and feel that soothing relaxation go down your back, down, down, down, to the lower part of your back, and those muscles let go and with every breath you inhale just feel your body drifting, floating, down deeper, down deeper, down deeper into total relaxation. Let your muscles go, relaxing more and more. Let all the muscles in your shoulders, running down your arms to your fingertips, relax. And let your arms feel so heavy, so heavy, so heavy, so comfortable, so relaxed. You may have tingling in your fingertips. That's perfectly fine. You may have warmth in the palms of your hands, and that's fine. And you may feel that you can barely lift your arms, they are so relaxed, they are so heavy, so heavy, so relaxed. And now you inhale once again and relax your chest muscles. And now as you exhale, feel your stomach muscles relax. As you exhale, relax all of the muscles in your stomach, let them go, and all of the muscles in your legs, feel them relax and all the muscles in your legs, so completely relaxed right to the tips of your toes. Notice how very comfortable your body feels, just drifting and floating, deeper, deeper, deeper relaxed. And as you are relaxing deeper and deeper, imagine a beautiful staircase. There are ten steps, and the steps lead you to a special and peaceful and beautiful place. In a moment you can begin to imagine taking a safe and gentle and easy step down, down, down on the staircase, leading you to a very peaceful, a very special place for you. You can imagine it to be any place you choose, perhaps you would enjoy a beach or ocean with clean, fresh air, or the mountains with a stream; any place is perfectly fine. In a moment I'm going to count backwards from ten to one and you can imagine taking the steps down and as you take each step, feel your body relax, more and more, feel it just drift down, down each step, and relax even deeper, ten, relax even deeper, nine . . . eight . . . seven . . . six . . . five . . . four . . . three . . . two . . . one . . . deeper, deeper, deeper, relaxed. And now imagine a peaceful and special place. You can imagine this special place and perhaps you can even feel it. You are in a [INSERT SPECIAL PLACE]. You are alone and there is no one to disturb you. This is the most peaceful place in the world for you. Imagine yourself there and feel that sense of peace flow through you and sense of well-being and enjoy these positive feelings and keep them with you long after this session is completed, for the rest of this day and evening, tomorrow. Allow these positive feelings to grow stronger and stronger, feeling at peace with a sense of well-being, and each and every time that you choose to do this kind of relaxation you will be able to relax deeper and deeper. Regardless of the stress and tension that may surround your life, you may now remain more at peace, more calm, more relaxed, and allow the tension and stresses to bounce off and away from you, just bounce off and away from you. And these positive feelings will stay with you and grow stronger and stronger throughout the day as you continue to relax deeper and deeper.

Enjoy your special place for another moment and then I will begin to count from one to ten and as I count from one to ten you can begin coming back to full alertness, and will feel refreshed and relaxed. Begin to come back now. One . . . two . . . coming up, three . . . four . . . five . . . six . . . seven . . . eight . . . nine, begin to open your eyes, and ten, open your eyes to a wide-awake, refreshed feeling.

Appendix II

Resource List

The following groups and agencies provide various types of help for victims of child abuse.

Hotlines

National Child Abuse Hotline
  (800) 422-4453
  Twenty-four-hour-a-day counseling and referrals.

Parents Anonymous Hotline
  (800) 421-0353 nationally, except in California
  (800) 352-0386 in California

Agency Assistance

Those who wish to receive help in a child-abuse situation can contact the following agencies.

Child Protective Services

Check your phone book for local listings, under *Department of Protective Services, Social and Rehabilitation Services* or *Department of Child and Family Services.* Every state has at least one agency that investigates child-abuse cases.

County Welfare Offices

Contact your local welfare office for assistance in reporting abuse.

United Way

For local United Way listings, look in the white pages of your phone book, under *Comprehensive Community Services, United Way Community Services,* or *Information Line.* You may also find a listing in the Yellow Pages, under *Social Services.*

Publications and Audiovisuals

National Center for Child Abuse
1205 Oneida St.
Denver, CO 80220
(303) 321-3963
Provides written materials and audovisuals on child abuse.

Legal Assistance

These agencies provide reporting information and information on the legal aspects of abuse.

National Center for Missing and Exploited Children
1835 K Street, N.W.
Washington, D.C. 20006
(202) 634-9821

National Committee for the Prevention of Child Abuse
332 South Michigan Ave.
Suite 950
Chicago, IL 60604-4357
(312) 663-3520

National Legal Resources Center for Child Advocacy and
  Protection
American Bar Association
1800 M St., N.W.
Washington, D.C. 20036
(202) 331-2250

SOURCE NOTES

Chapter 1: "I Thought I Was the Only One"

1. *National Study of the Incidence and Severity of Child Abuse and Neglect,* U.S. Children's Bureau, DHHS publication no. (OHDS) 81–30325, 23.

2. J. H. Gagnon and W. Simon, *Sexual Encounters Between Adults and Children,* cited in ibid.

3. Jon Conte, "Progress in Treating the Sexual Abuse of Children," *Social Work* (May-June, 1984), 258–262.

4. David Finkelhor, *Sexually Victimized Children* (New York: Free Press, 1979), 88.

5. Geraldine Faria and Nancy Belohlavek, "Treating Female Adult Survivors of Childhood Incest," *Social Casework: The Journal of Contemporary Social Work* (Family Service America, 1984), 465, 471.

6. Mary De Young, *Incest: An Annotated Bibliography* (Jefferson, N.C.: McFarland, 1985), 71, 81, 91, 103–107.

7. *National Study.*

8. Blair Justice and Rita Justice, *The Broken Taboo: Sex in the Family* (New York: Human Sciences Press, 1979).

9. Mary Lou Hyde and Phyllis A. Kaufman, "Women Molested as Children: Therapeutic and Legal Issues in Civil Actions," *American Journal of Forensic Psychiatry,* no. 4 (1984): 147–157.

10. James C. Coleman and James N. Butcher, *Abnormal Psychology and Modern Life* (Glenview, Ill.: Scott, Foresman, 1984), 63–64.

Chapter 2: "How Do I Know if I'm a Victim?"

1. Karin C. Meiselman, *Incest: A Psychological Study of Causes and Effects With Treatment Recommendations* (San Francisco: Jossey-Bass, 1978).

2. Selma Brown, "Clinical Illustrations of the Sexual Misuse of Girls," *Child Welfare,* no. 58 (July/August 1979): 435–442.

3. National Committee for Prevention of Child Abuse, *Basic Facts About Child Abuse* (1982).

4. Roland Summit and JoAnn Kryso, "Sexual Abuse of Children: A Clinical Spectrum," *American Journal of Orthopsychiatry,* no. 48 (1978): 237–251.

5. Jacqueline Carroll et al., "Family Experiences of Self-mutilating Patients," *American Journal of Psychiatry,* no. 137 (July 1980): 852–853.

6. Carl P. Malmquist, Thomas J. Kiresuk, and Robert M. Spano, "Personality Characteristics of Women With Repeated Illegitimacies: Descriptive Aspects," *American Journal of Orthopsychiatry,* no. 36 (1966): 476–484.

7. P. P. Vitaliano, D. Boyer, and J. James, "Perceptions of Juvenile Experience: Females Involved in Prostitution Versus Property Offenders," *Criminal Justice and Behavior,* no. 8 (September 1981): 325–342.

8. Jody Yeary, "Incest and Chemical Dependency," *Journal of Psychoactive Drugs,* no. 14 (January-June 1982): 133–135.

9. Judith L. Herman, "Father-Daughter Incest," *Professional Psychology,* no. 12 (1981), 76–80.

10. Vicki Saltman and Robert Solomon, "Incest and Multiple Personality," part 2, *Psychological Reports,* no. 50, (1982): 1127–1141.

11. Harold Levitan, "Explicit Incestuous Motifs in Psychosomatic Patients," *Psychotherapy and Psychosomatics,* no. 37 (1982): 22–25.

12. Judith L. Herman and Lisa Hirschman, "Father-Daughter Incest," *Journal of Women in Culture and Society,* no. 4 (1977): 735–756.

13. Marvin Hersko et al, "Incest: A Three Way Process," *Journal of Social Therapy,* no. 7 (1966): 22–31.

14. Karin C. Meiselman, "Personality Characteristics of Incest History Psychotherapy Patients: A Research Note," *Archives of Sexual Behavior,* no. 9 (1980): 195–197.

15. S. Van Buskirk and C. Cole, "Characteristics of Eight Women Seeking Therapy for the Effects of Incest," *Psychotherapy: Theory, Research and Practice,* no. 20 (1983).

16. William James, *Principles of Psychology,* cited in Stanley Coopersmith, *The Antecedents of Self-esteem* (San Francisco: W. H. Freeman & Co., 1967), 28–33.

17. George H. Mead, *Mind, Self and Society,* cited in Coopersmith, *Antecedents,* 28–33.

18. Coopersmith, *Antecedents,* 38–44.

19. Andre Godin and Mónegul Hallez, "Paternal Images and Divine Paternity," *From Religious Experience to Religious Attitude,* ed. A. Godin (Chicago: Loyola Univ. Press, 1965), 75–89.

20. Material from Harborview Sexual Assault Center, Seattle, Washington.

21. Dr. Paul Meier, "Personality Disorders" (class notes of seminar at Western Conservative Baptist Seminary, Portland, Oregon, June 9–13, 1986).

22. Paul D. Meier, *Christian Child Rearing and Personality Development* (Grand Rapids, Mich.: Baker Book House, 1977).

Chapter 3: Recognizing Offender Behavior

1. "Personality Characteristics of Offenders, Normals and Victims" (Seattle, Wash.: Harborville Sexual Assault Center).

2. Svend Riemer, "A Research Note on Incest," *American Journal of Sociology,* no. 45 (1940): 566–575.

3. Tamar Cohen, "The Incestuous Family Revisited," *Social Casework,* no. 64 (March 1983): 154–161.

4. Bruno M. Cormier, Miriam Kennedy, and Jadurga Sangowicz, "Psychodynamics of Father-Daughter Incest," *Canadian Psychiatric Association Journal,* no. 7 (October 1962): 203–217.

5. Mary De Young, *Incest: An Annotated Bibliography* (Jefferson, N.C.: McFarland, 1985).

6. James C. Coleman and James N. Butcher, *Abnormal Psychology and Modern Life* (Glenview, Ill.: Scott, Foresman, 1984), 233.

7. Dr. Paul Meier, "Personality Disorders" (class notes of seminar at Western Conservative Baptist Seminary, Portland, Oregon, June 9–13, 1986).

8. Paul D. Meier et al, *Introduction to Psychology and Counseling* (Grand Rapids, Mich.: Baker Book House, 1982), 225–229.

9. Meier et al, *Introduction to Psychology*, 225–229.

10. Ibid.

11. Joyce Spencer, "Father-Daughter Incest: A Clinical View From the Corrections Field," *Child Welfare*, no. 57 (November 1981): 581–589.

12. Coleman and Butcher, *Abnormal Psychology*, 239.

13. Ibid., 241.

14. Meier et al, *Introduction to Psychology*, 321–322.

15. Narcyz Lukianowicz, "Incest I: Paternal Incest; Incest II: Other Types of Incest," *British Journal of Psychiatry*, no. 120 (March 1972): 301–313.

16. Dr. Paul D. Meier, "Personality Disorders" (class notes of seminar at Western Conservative Baptist Seminary, Portland, Oregon, June 9–13, 1986).

17. Karen D. Kirkland and Chris A. Bauer, "MMPI Traits of Incestuous Fathers," *Journal of Clinical Psychology*, no. 38 (July 1979): 645–649.

18. Robert E. Longo, "Learning and Experience Among Adolescent Sexual Offenders," *International Journal of Offender Therapy and Comparative Criminology*, no. 26, 3:235–241.

19. A. Nicholas Groth, "Sexual Trauma in the Life Histories of Rapists and Child Molesters," *Victimology: An International Journal*, no. 4, (1979).

20. S. Kirson Weinberg, *Incest Behavior* (New York: Citadel Press, 1955), 94–120.

21. W. E. Prendergast, "The Sex Offender: How to Spot Him Before It's Too Late," *Sexology*, 46–51.

Chapter 4: Recognizing Offender Thinking

1. Adapted from Samuel Yochelson and Stanton Samenow, *The Criminal Personality: A Profile for Change,* vol. 1 (New York: Jason Aronson, 1976), 252–253.
2. Ibid., 254.
3. Information compiled by Children's Services Division, Portland, Oregon, based upon Yochelson and Samenow's work.
4. Yochelson and Samenow, *Criminal Personality,* 258.

Chapter 5: How Do Offenders Groom Their Victims?

1. Linda Gordon and Paul O'Keefe, "Incest as a Form of Family Violence: Evidence From Historical Case Records," *Journal of Marriage and the Family,* no. 46 (February 1984): 27–34.
2. Information received from Children's Services Division, Portland, Oregon.
3. Judith L. Herman and Lisa Hirschman, "Families at Risk for Father-Daughter Incest," *American Journal of Psychiatry,* no. 138 (July 1981): 967–970.
4. Noel Lustig et al, "Incest: A Family Group Survival Pattern," *Archives of General Psychology,* no. 14 (January 1966): 31–40.
5. Harold I. Eist and Adeline U. Mandel, "Family Treatment of Ongoing Incest Behavior," *Family Process,* no. 7 (September 1968): 216–232.
6. Robin Norwood, *Women Who Love Too Much* (Los Angeles: J. P. Tarcher, 1985), 8.
7. Blair Justice and Rita Justice, *The Broken Taboo: Sex in the Family* (New York: Human Sciences Press, 1979).
8. Mary De Young, "Promises, Threats and Lies: Keeping Incest Secret," *Journal of Humanics,* no. 9 (May 1981): 61–71.
9. Thomas G. Gutheil and Nicholas C. Avery, "Multiple Overt Incest as Family Defense Against Loss," *Family Process,* no. 16 (March 1977): 105–116.
10. Information compiled from Children's Services Division,

Portland, Oregon, and Harborview Sexual Assault Center, Seattle, Washington.

Chapter 6: "Why Didn't Anyone Try to Save Me?"

1. *World's Greatest Fairy Tales* (Danbury Press), 81–83.
2. M. De Young, ed., *Incest: An Annotated Bibliography* (Jefferson, N.C.: McFarland, 1985).
3. Ibid.
4. Ibid.
5. Ibid. Blair Justice and Rita Justice, *The Broken Taboo: Sex in the Family* (New York: Human Sciences Press, 1979), 139–152.
6. De Young, *Sexual Victimization.*
7. Justice and Justice, *Taboo.*
8. Parents United.
9. Noel Lustig et al, "Incest: A Family Group Survival Pattern," *Archives of General Psychiatry,* no. 14 (January 1966): 31–40.
10. S. Kirson Weinberg, *Incest Behavior* (New York: Citadel, 1955), 67–81.
11. Jerome A. Kroth, *Child Sexual Abuse: Analysis of a Family Therapy Approach* (Springfield, Ill.: Charles C. Thomas, 1979), 104–118.
12. M. De Young, "Siblings of Oedipus: Brothers and Sisters of Incest Victims," *Child Welfare,* no. 60 (September/October 1981): 561–568.
13. Lord W. Heims and Irving Kaufman, "Variations on a Theme of Incest," *American Journal of Orthopsychiatry,* no. 33 (1963): 311–312.
14. C. S. Lewis, *The Problem of Pain* (New York: Macmillan, 1962).

Chapter 7: Surviving the Betrayal of Childhood

1. Susan S. Van Buskirk and Carolyn F. Cole, "Characteristics of Eight Women Seeking Therapy for the Effects of Incest,"

Psychotherapy: Theory, Research and Practice, no. 20 (Winter 1983): 503–514.

2. Ibid.

3. Judith L. Herman and L. Hirschman, "Father-Daughter Incest," *Journal of Women in Culture and Society,* no. 4, 2: 735–756. Judith L. Herman, *Father-Daughter Incest* (Cambridge, Mass.: Harvard Univ. Press, 1982), 67–95. Karin C. Meiselman, *Incest: A Psychological Study of Causes and Effects With Treatment Recommendations* (San Francisco: Jossey-Bass, 1978).

4. Herman and Hirschman, "Father-Daughter Incest" S. Brown, "Clinical Illustrations of the Sexual Misuse of Girls," *Child Welfare,* no. 58 (July/August 1979): 435–442.

5. George Thorman, *Incestuous Families* (Springfield, Ill.: Charles C. Thomas, 1983).

6. J. B. Thompkins, "Penis Envy and Incest: A Case Report," *Psychoanalytic Review,* no. 27 (1940): 319–325. Brown, "Sexual Misuse."

7. Brown, "Sexual Misuse," 435–442.

Chapter 8: Giving Yourself the Right to Grieve

1. Paul D. Meier et al, *Introduction to Psychology and Counseling* (Grand Rapids, Mich.: Baker Book House, 1982), 266–268.

2. Ibid.

3. David G. Benner, ed., *Baker Encyclopedia of Psychology* (Grand Rapids, Mich.: Baker Book House, 1985), 472–474.

4. Information on loss compiled by Dr. Carol Clifton, Western Psychological Services Center, Portland, Oregon.

5. Meier et al, *Introduction to Psychology,* 266–268.

6. Paul Tournier, *A Doctor's Casebook in the Light of the Bible* (New York: Harper & Row, 1960), 64–70.

7. Benner, *Baker Encyclopedia,* 472–474.

8. Ibid.

9. Ibid.

10. Meier et al, *Introduction to Psychology,* 266–268.

11. Clifton, information on loss.

12. Benner, *Baker Encyclopedia*, 473.

13. C. S. Lewis, *A Grief Observed* (New York: Bantam, 1976).

Chapter 9: Airing the Wounds

1. Compiled from Henry Giaretto, *Integrated Treatment of Child Sexual Abuse* (Palo Alto, Calif.: Science & Behavior Books, 1982).

2. H. Norman Wright, *The Christian Use of Emotional Power* (Old Tappan, N.J.: Fleming H. Revell, 1974), 112.

3. Giaretto, *Integrated Treatment*.

4. Information compiled from various sources by Dr. Carol Clifton, Western Psychological Services Center, Portland, Oregon.

Chapter 10: Getting the Big Picture

1. Mary De Young, ed., *Incest: An Annotated Bibliography* (Jefferson, N.C.: McFarland, 1985).

2. Noel Lustig et al, "Incest: A Family Group Survival Pattern," *Archives of General Psychology,* no. 14 (January 1966): 31–40.

3. Thomas G. Gutheil and Nicholas C. Avery, "Multiple Overt Incest as Family Defense Against Loss," *Family Process,* no. 16 (March 1977): 105–116.

4. *Webster's New Collegiate Dictionary* (Springfield, Mass.: G. & C. Merriam, 1975).

5. David Augsberger, *Caring Enough to Confront* (Ventura, Calif.: Regal Books, 1973), 11–15.

6. Ibid.

Chapter 11: The Road of Healing

1. K. Lampson, *Indicators of Recovery* (unpublished handout, 1984).

2. 1986 Fall Workshop on Women Molested as Children, Lutheran Family Services, Portland, Oregon.

Chapter 12: Counsel for Loved Ones

1. Judith L. Herman, *Father-Daughter Incest* (Cambridge, Mass.: Harvard Univ. Press, 1982), 177–220.
2. David B. Peters, *Betrayal of Innocence* (Waco, Tex: Word Books, 1986), 90.
3. Ibid., 93.
4. Ibid., 96–97.
5. Ibid., 100.
6. Ibid., 100–102.
7. Ibid., 102.
8. Ibid., 103.
9. Ibid., 103.
10. Ibid., 104.
11. Ibid., 104–105.
12. Gary Strudler, *Shout It Out* (Portland, Ore.: Children's Council of the Junior League, 1985), 5.
13. Ibid., 39.

Chapter 13: What About the Christian Offender?

1. Joyce Spencer, "Father-Daughter Incest: A Clinical View From the Corrections Field," *Child Welfare,* no. 57 (November 1981): 581–598.
2. B. Delen, *The Sex Offender* (Boston: Beacon Press, 1978), .
3. Karin C. Meiselman, *Incest: A Psychological Study of Causes and Effects With Treatment Recommendations* (San Francisco: Jossey-Bass, 1978).
4. Paul H. Gebhard et al, *Sex Offenders: An Analysis of Types* (New York: Harper & Row, 1965), 269.
5. Samuel Yochelson and Stanton Samenow, *The Criminal Personality: A Profile for Change,* vol. 1 (New York: Jason Aronson, 1976), 288–289.